MEDITERRANEAN DIET FOR BEGINNERS:

A COMPLETE MEAL PLAN FOR YOUR 2020. DISCOVER TASTY AND LIGHT RECIPES FOR BALANCING YOUR DIET AND LIVE A HEALTHY LIFE

DEANNA BURNS

ALL RIGHTS RESERVED.

This book contains material protected under international and Federal Copyright Laws and Treaties. Any unauthorized reprint or use of this material is prohibited.

No part of this book may be reproduced or transmitted in any form or by any means, electronic or mechanical, including photocopying, recording, or by any information storage and retrieval system without express written permission from the author/publisher.

TABLE OF CONTENTS

INTRODUCTION 6

CHAPTER 1   WHY THE MEDITERRANEAN DIET? 11

    10-Day Diet Meal Plan 19

CHAPTER 2   BREAKFAST 21

1) Breakfast Egg on Avocado 21
2) Breakfast Egg-artichoke Casserole 23
3) Brekky Egg-potato Hash 25
4) Dill and Tomato Frittata 26
5) Mediterranean Egg White Breakfast Sandwich 26
6) Mediterranean Breakfast Casserole 29
7) Gingerbread Breakfast Quinoa Bake with Banana 30
8) Egg Muffins with Vegetables and Feta Cheese 31
9) Mediterranean Breakfast Stir Fry (Melamen) 32
10) Mediterranean Pistachios and Fruits with Yogurt 33
11) Mediterranean Eggs 34
12) Shakshuka 36
13) Veggie wrap 37
14) Tiganites 38
15) Greek Olive and Feta Cheese Pasta 39
16) Tomatoes Stuffed with Goat Cheese 40
17) Cucumber Yogurt Salad 41
18) Savory Greek White Fava Bean Salad 41
19) Tangy Orange Roasted Asparagus Salad 42
20) Romano cheese preferably grated 42
21) Mediterranean Mixed Greens 43
22) Creamy Paninis 45
23) Scrambled eggs 46

CHAPTER 3   LUNCH 42

24) Favorite Pepper Soup 42
25) The Mediterranean Tomato Soup 43
26) Authentic Yogurt and Cucumber Salad 44
27) Delightful Pesto Pizza 45
28) Linguine Dredged in Tomato Clam Sauce 46
29) Wild Mushrooms and Pork Chops 47
30) Mediterranean Lamb Chops 48
31) Mushroom and Beef Risotto 49
32) Broiled Mushrooms Burgers and Goat Cheese 50
33) Tuna and Potato Salad 51
34) Parmesan and Chicken Veggie 52
35) Mushroom and Pork Chops 53

36) Oven Roasted Garlic Chicken Thigh 54
37) Trout with Wilted Greens 55

CHAPTER 4   SALAD 56

38) Easy Grilled Chicken Salad 56
39) Light and Fresh Arugula Salad .. 57
40) Mediterranean Greens 57
41) Pear salad with creamy yogurt dressing 58
42) Anchovy and Orange Salad 58
43) Asian Peanut Sauce Over Noodle Salad 59
44) Blue Cheese and Arugula Salad . 60
45) Classic Greek Salad 61
46) Cucumber Salad Japanese Style . 62
47) Simple Mixed Herb Salad 63
48) Delicious Bread Salad 64

CHAPTER 5   FISH 65

49) Fish and Orzo 65
50) Baked Sea Bass 66
51) Fish and Tomato Sauce 66
52) Halibut and Quinoa Mix 67
53) Lemon and Dates Barramundi 68
54) Fish Cakes 69
55) Catfish Fillets and Rice 69
56) Halibut Pan 70
57) Baked Shrimp Mix 71
58) Shrimp and Lemon Sauce 72
59) Shrimp and Beans Salad 72
60) Pecan Salmon Fillets 73
61) Salmon and Broccoli 74
62) Salmon and Peach Pan 74
63) Tarragon Cod Fillets 75
64) Salmon and Radish Mix 76
65) Smoked Salmon and Watercress Salad 76
66) Salmon and Corn Salad 77
67) Cod and Mushrooms Mix 78
68) Sesame Shrimp Mix 78
69) Creamy Curry Salmon 79
70) Mahi Mahi and Pomegranate Sauce 79
71) Smoked Salmon and Veggies Mix 80

CHAPTER 6   VEGETABLE 81

72) Vegetable Stew 81
73) Parmesan Broccoli 82
74) Roasted Vegetable Salad 82
75) Fried Green Tomatoes 83
76) One-of-a-Kind Veggie Slaw 84
77) Ratatouille Grilled Style 85
78) Roasted Root Veggie 86
79) Stuffed Sweet Potato 87

CHAPTER 7   MEAT 89

80) Mediterranean Grilled Pork Chops 89
81) Simple Pork Stir Fry 90
82) Pork and Lentil Soup 91
83) Simple Braised Pork 92
84) Pork and Chickpea Stew 93

- 85) Pork and Greens Salad 94
- 86) Pork Strips and Rice 95
- 87) Slow Cooked Mediterranean Pork 96
- 88) Pork and Bean Stew 96
- 89) Pork with Couscous 98
- 90) Easy Roasted Pork Shoulder 99
- 91) Herb Roasted Pork 99
- 92) Slow Cooked Beef Brisket 100
- 93) Mediterranean Beef Dish 101
- 94) Beef Tartar 101
- 95) Meatballs and Sauce 102

CHAPTER 8 DESSERT 104

- 96) Cold Lemon Squares 104
- 97) Blackberry and Apples Cobbler 104
- 98) Black Tea Cake 105
- 99) Green Tea and Vanilla Cream ... 106
- 100) Blueberry Frozen Yogurt 106
- 101) Delectable Strawberry Popsicle 107
- 102) Deliciously Cold Lychee Sorbet 108
- 103) Easy Fruit Compote 108
- 104) Five Berry Mint Orange Infusion 109
- 105) Greek Yogurt Muesli Parfaits . 110
- 106) Mediterranean Baked Apples ... 110
- 107) Spiced Pear with Applesauce 111
- 108) Cherry Clafoutis 111
- 109) Stuffed Figs 112

CHAPTER 9 HEALTH BENEFITS OF THE MEDITERRANEAN DIET 113

CHAPTER 10 INSIDER SECRETS TO REACHING DIET SUCCESS 120

How to Stay Hydrated 120
Vitamins and Supplements 122
Meal Preparation and Portion Planning 122
Tracking Your Macronutrients 124
Counting Calories and Forming a Deficit 126

CHAPTER 11 FREQUENTLY ASKED QUESTIONS 128

CONCLUSION 137

Introduction

Since the time of the Seven Countries Study, there have been hundreds of research studies on the Mediterranean diet. The diet is associated with the maintenance of your general health. Although scientists are not sure about the exact quantities of various foods that people should aim for, the general principles of the Mediterranean diet are well established. Studies have shown that it reduces the risk of virtually every chronic disease that is now said to plague western society, including heart disease, stroke, diabetes, cancer, and even Alzheimer's disease and other types of dementia.

Recent studies have shown the superiority of the Mediterranean diet as compared to a low-fat diet. In the Pretimed study by J. Salas-Salvado and colleagues, several hundred adults without diabetes were followed for several years in order to determine whether different diets could reduce the risk of developing diabetes. Study participants were divided into three groups. The first group followed a traditional Mediterranean diet with an emphasis on the consumption of extra virgin olive oil. The second group followed a Mediterranean diet but consumed extra servings of nuts. This was done because many nuts contain the same types of fats as olive oil does, and they also contain high amounts of fiber. The third group consumed a low-fat diet of the type that was in vogue in the United States from the 1960s onward.

It was found that although a Mediterranean diet cannot prevent the development of type 2 diabetes, it significantly reduces the risk. About 10% of people following the Mediterranean developed type 2 diabetes after being on a diet for 5 years. However, nearly 18% of people following the low-fat diet ended up diabetic. The study only went on for five years, but as time went on the differences between the diets were widening. The study showed that with regards to the development of diabetes, whether you consume nuts or olive oil was not important. The main benefit came from following the general principles of the Mediterranean diet.

Keep in mind that the standard American diet was not used in this study. It is well established that doing nothing and eating typical western diets significantly increases the risk of developing type 2 diabetes, even compared to the low-fat diet that Salas-Salvado used as the control diet in their studies. This means that if you transition to a Mediterranean diet from a low-fat diet, you are going to see very large reductions in your risk of developing type 2 diabetes. Overall, it is believed that following a Mediterranean diet will reduce the risk that you'll develop type 2 diabetes by around 21%.

In fact, if you are overweight and follow the Mediterranean diet closely while maintaining reasonable portion sizes, you can even reverse type 2 diabetes if you are able to achieve significant weight loss. If you are pre-diabetic or diabetic (type 2), you should be looking for a weight loss of about 25% of your current body weight in order to achieve these types of results. People who can do this often find they are able to reduce their medications and, in some cases, even get off their medications altogether.

The Mediterranean diet has also been shown to reduce "bad" or LDL cholesterol. Before we get to the study results, let's briefly review the different types of lipids, or fats, that are present in your bloodstream. Everyone has heard about cholesterol, but there are two types of cholesterol that you must worry about. LDL cholesterol is the dangerous type. It can become stuck to your artery walls, and when it does this, it will lead to the formation of plaque or hardening of the arteries over time and the formation of clots. Basically, this is a problem of probability. So, the more LDL cholesterol you have in your blood, the more likely it is to get stuck and cause problems. Medical scientists generally recommend that you have low total cholesterol, 200 mg/dL or below. However, it's really LDL that they are worried about, and ideally, an LDL level of 100 mg/dL or lower is desirable, especially if you are pre-diabetic or you have type 2 diabetes. If you have no other health problems, most medical professionals believe it is OK to have an LDL level up to 129 mg/dL.

The level of LDL cholesterol in your blood is directly associated with the amount of saturated fat that you consume in your diet. Saturated fat comes mainly from animal sources such as red meat, pork fat, and poultry skin. If you consume 20 mg or less of saturated fat per day, you can lower your LDL cholesterol quickly. The best way to do this is by following the Mediterranean diet, which will lower your saturated fat intake without having to think about it. Keep in mind that there are some plant sources of saturated fat as well that should be avoided if you are following a Mediterranean diet. These include coconut oil and palm oil.

If you cannot control your LDL cholesterol with diet, your doctor may put you on a statin drug. Red yeast rice, which is a natural statin available over the counter, can also be used to lower LDL cholesterol levels. However, keep in mind that red yeast rice can be contaminated with toxic substances that may lead to the development of cancer. Check with the manufacturer to see if they screen for this.

The second type of cholesterol is HDL, which is known as the "good cholesterol". HDL cholesterol basically acts as a cleanup system in your bloodstream. It's got two roles. The first role is to collect excess LDL from your bloodstream and return it to the liver, where it can be processed. So, for this reason, people that have higher levels of HDL cholesterol tend to have lower levels of LDL cholesterol.

HDL plays a second, very important role in the body. It not only reduces the amount of LDL in your bloodstream, it helps clean the walls of the arteries, keeping them healthy and free of clots. The minimum level of HDL that medical doctors consider healthy is 40 mg/dL, but the higher the better. Unfortunately, efforts to find a drug that will raise HDL have failed. Also, there doesn't appear to be any specific diet that will raise HDL cholesterol. However, there is one way that you can influence your HDL levels, and that is by losing weight and maintaining some level of physical activity. If you are significantly overweight or obese, then losing 20% of your body weight or more may increase your HDL levels. Regular exercise has also been shown to modestly improve HDL levels. A level of 50 mg/dL or higher is thought to be protective against cardiovascular disease.

The ratio of LDL to HDL cholesterol has been shown to be a good indicator of heart disease risk. Let's say that you had the minimum levels of LDL and HDL thought to be protective. For LDL cholesterol, that would be 100 mg/dL. For HDL cholesterol, that would be 40 mg/dL. The ratio would then be 100/40 = 2.5. For this reason, a ratio of 2.5 or less is indicative of a low cardiovascular risk. Anything below that is desirable. If your ratio is above that, then you probably have some work to do.

So how does the Mediterranean diet perform when it comes to lowering LDL cholesterol and improving this ratio? As you might expect, since people on the Mediterranean diet consume less saturated fat, they have lower levels of LDL cholesterol. In a significant study done by F. Montserrat, people following the standard Mediterranean diet with large amounts of extra virgin olive oil were compared to people on a Mediterranean diet + nuts and people following the standard low-fat diet recommended by cardiologists.

Surprisingly, the low-fat diet barely reduced LDL cholesterol levels. The average reduction was only 2-3 points. So, if you entered the stud with an LDL cholesterol level of say 129 mg/dL, following a low-fat diet for six months might drop your level to 127 mg/dL. The amount of reduction is not considered significant.

The Mediterranean diet, however, significantly lowers LDL cholesterol over a short time period. Montserrat found that when combined with high amounts of extra virgin olive oil, it could reduce LDL cholesterol by 10 points on average in just three months of dieting. Following the Mediterranean diet with nuts also reduced LDL cholesterol levels, but by only 6.5 points on average. This shows the important role that olive oil can play in maintaining good health.

Why the Mediterranean diet?

There are no counting calories! This is one of those positives that people love about the Mediterranean diet. So many new diets restrict people on a calorie basis which can be quite frustrating and often detrimental to your health if you require a greater caloric intake for your physical and health needs. If you're required to count calories, you must be very careful to remember every little thing you're eating as a snack, or even adding on your dishes like dressing or cheese. The Mediterranean diet offers a great amount of flexibility regarding this because it's shifting you away from unhealthy food choices to healthier ones. Of course, you should be aware of your dietary choices and avoid overeating, but you also have the freedom to decide on your portion sizes which means you can take an extra few veggies if you'd like, or you can skip having a snack if you're not feeling hungry. The idea is to eat more filling meals that will ensure you aren't feeling hungry other than at mealtimes. By cutting out the sugar, junk food, and fast food from your diet and loading up on fiber from fruits, vegetables, and whole grains, you're eating healthier without having to worry about every item's calorie count.

You can have wine! If you're someone who already enjoys a glass of wine to unwind after a long day, this is going to be an aspect you love about the Mediterranean diet. You get to have that glass of wine and feel good that it is allowed on your diet and can have heart-healthy properties. Recent research on red wine has found that it is high in antioxidants that may prevent cardiovascular heart disease. The people of the Mediterranean also enjoyed having red wine with a meal so it could tentatively be linked to their excellent cardiovascular health. But it's important to note many warnings regarding alcohol consumption. The Mediterranean diet encourages "moderate consumption," which means there are limits in place. Healthy men can drink 2 glasses a day. Healthy women may have up to 1 glass a day. Also, these possible health benefits are only associated with red wine - not other alcoholic beverages or hard liquor. If you're an avid drinker of those and hoping to substitute that for wine in your Mediterranean diet, that won't work! Before incorporating alcohol into your diet, you should speak to your doctor to ensure it does not interfere with your health, family history, if you're pregnant or breastfeeding, or any medication you may be taking. You don't have to be drinking wine to gain the benefits of the diet, but if you are a drinker, then you're going to love this diet even more!

The Mediterranean diet is full of fiber-rich foods so you will feel full for longer. Some diets will often restrict the amount of carbohydrates, fruit or vegetable that you can eat due to worries about too much glucose production from carbs, or natural sugars contained in fruit. Thankfully, the Mediterranean diet does no such thing! And that's a good thing because it allows you to have a diet full of fibrous foods. Beans, whole grains, lentils, and fresh vegetables are rich in fiber which is great for your body. Fiber keeps you feeling full for a longer period which means you are less likely to snack in between meals. That means fewer calories and more weight loss! Not only that, some diets can truly have a damaging effect on your digestive system causing constipation or diarrhea due to changes in your regular fiber intake. With the Mediterranean diet, having this high intake of fiber will keep your digestive tract functioning smoothly and keep your bowel movements regular. That means less chance of gastrointestinal or rectal problems. Fiber also gives you energy which is why many people will try and have whole grains for breakfast, such as whole grain cereal, whole wheat bread, or whole grain oatmeal.

This diet will improve your mental alertness. The Mediterranean diet removes all the processed and unhealthy substances from your diet such as refined grains, soda, fast food, trans fats, and junk food. That can be tough to do, but the results it brings are very beneficial for your body and mind. All these sugary treats would cause spikes in your blood sugar and cause a rush of insulin throughout the body. That brings around symptoms like mood swings, false hunger pants, irritability, fatigue, and weakness. Instead of keeping you mentally alert, those foods slow you down and distract you from working at your best potential. When following the Mediterranean diet, you are replacing the processed sugars with fresh vegetables and fruits that are full of healthy minerals like vitamin B, folic acid, potassium, vitamin D, omega 3 fatty acids, and more! This keeps the body functioning in top mental and cognitive functioning which gives you more alertness, focus, memory recall, and concentration.

You can have fruit which is great to satisfy your sweet tooth! Many diets forbid you from eating fruit because of their natural sugars and the net carbs that they could add to your daily caloric intake. This can be quite tough, especially if you're already giving up artificial and refined sugar. Sometimes, your sweet tooth just needs to be satisfied! The more you must give up, often the more tempting it will be to reach for those same ingredients! With the Mediterranean diet, you're encouraged to make fruit a healthy dessert option. Instead of unhealthy sugary snacks, fruit should be your go-to. Whether it's juicy watermelon, a ripe banana, or sweet berries, these natural sugars are much less harmful to your body than artificial ones. Portion size is important, so you don't want to go overboard, but many people are happy to have this option as a sweet treat!

It's very easy to adjust if you're eating outside of your home. One of the worries when you're dieting is feeling constrained if you're ever outside the comfort of your own home at mealtimes. Especially if your diet requires specialized ingredients without a lot of freedom in making meal choices at restaurants or at a friend's house. You may be panicking and wondering how to adjust.

With the Mediterranean diet, it's very easy to do just that! Let's say you're out at dinner with friends. What can you order that would fit the requirements of the Mediterranean diet? Most places will offer a seafood option so you can have your choice of fish, lobster, shrimp, or crab! If there isn't a seafood choice, you can pick a poultry option - just be sure to avoid red meat! You can also pick a side of fresh vegetables or a small salad. When it comes to dessert, be sure to go for the most natural and organic option instead of a baked good full of refined sugar. You can ask for fresh fruit, or maybe an organic smoothie. The ease and flexibility that the Mediterranean diet allows even when you are outside of the home and away from your prepared meals is what makes it such a favorite among its followers. There's no panic about breaking your diet or making an unhealthy food choice.

There's so much delicious variety to choose from in the Mediterranean diet. This is not a diet you will get bored of easily or feel like the food choice is restricting. There is so much that you can eat and so many foods and recipes you can try. Remember, the Mediterranean region includes countries like Greece, Turkey, Spain, Italy, Morocco and many more! So, there are always new recipes and ethnic foods that you can include in your menu. Maybe by experimenting, you'll find a new favorite! Not only that, there are great varieties of protein that you can incorporate in your dishes, as well as vegetables, whole grains, poultry, and the occasional meal of red meat. You're also encouraged to use spices, fresh herbs, and olive oil to add flavor to your meal which gives it another depth of flavor. With many avenues of exploration, you will not feel constrained by this diet or feel like you're running out of things to eat. Of course, there are clear items you should avoid like trans fats, sugar, and processed foods, but focusing on what you can eat will allow you to enjoy your meals so much more and be excited for the next one!

There will be no harmful side effects that often occur when you reduce your intake of carbohydrates. Many diets lately have been embracing the concept of low carbohydrate intake believing it causes blood sugar spikes and wanting to guide the body through a different fat-burning process called ketosis. The keto diet and other low carb diets drastically reduce the number of carbohydrates you're consuming a day. This can be a quick method to reduce weight, but it can bring a tough adjustment period for the body which includes symptoms like weakness, fatigue, diarrhea, muscle cramps, nausea, and other things that could interfere with your health and daily life. These are temporary, but they could still last a matter of weeks as your body adjusts. That's because carbohydrates tend to make up more than half of our diet. Cutting it down to something very minimal like 5% of your daily intake can be tough on your body! The Mediterranean diet embraces the concept of whole grains because they are healthier for you than refined carbohydrates. They're full of fiber and vitamin B12 and keep you feeling full. Whole grains tend to be lower on the glycemic index compared to refined grains. That means they will not cause blood sugar spikes. This allows you to have a more natural place for whole grains in your diet and still feel confident that you are gaining the health benefits they provide. Cutting something completely from your diet, especially something you will encounter all the time in your food choices, can be very tough and make them seem more tempting!

You don't have to become a gym rat! One of the things that people also love about the Mediterranean diet is that it doesn't require intense exercise that some diets will encourage. This makes it appealing to people of all health levels and physical fitness. It simply encourages you to incorporate more physical activity into your routine, whether that's a walk around the block, a swim session at the pool, or jogging or biking. You don't have to join an array of gym classes or feel like you're not doing enough to burn calories. The people of the Mediterranean very naturally fit exercise into their daily life and activities.

They didn't end up dreading it or getting burned out which can often happen if you're following a diet where you must devote too much time at the gym. Instead, try and make the choices to be more active voluntarily, such as taking the stairs instead of the elevator, or parking your car a few blocks away and enjoying the walk to work. This way, you're still burning calories which means you're keeping yourself healthy and losing weight at the same time!

What You Can and Cannot Eat

As with any diet, it's important to begin and plan your menu by knowing exactly what you can and cannot eat. That means knowing what's on your "allowed" list and what's on your "forbidden" list. The more informed you are, the less likely you will make a mistake and bring home something you shouldn't eat!

What You Should Be Eating Most Often:

> Vegetables: Vegetables are highly encouraged on the Mediterranean diet for the vitamins and minerals they carry, as well as fiber to keep you feeling full. Try and buy fresh vegetables, but frozen is also a good substitute. Be careful about buying canned veggies because they often are high in sodium. Be sure it's a low sodium version so you are not consuming extra salt. Ginger and garlic are considered staples in the Mediterranean diet because of the way they enhance the flavor of food and have anti-inflammatory health benefits.

Examples) tomatoes, potatoes, green beans, bell peppers, broccoli, carrots, mushrooms, olives, squash, zucchini, spinach, kale, onions

> Fish and Seafood: This should be your main source of protein on the Mediterranean diet. You should try and include this in your diet at least two times a week - but more! It is a great source of protein that will not increase your risk of heart disease, along with a high intake of omega 3 fatty acids

which have been discovered to be essential for our health. There are many types of fish you can try including fatty fishes like tuna and white fish like salmon and mackerel. Try and cook them as naturally as you can and avoid fatty batters or deep frying. Simple herbs and spices should enhance the flavor.

Examples) tuna, salmon, mackerel, sardines, anchovies, clams, oysters, shrimp, lobster, mussels, crab

> Legumes and Beans: These are another great source of protein that is often overlooked. But they are full of fiber too! Not only that, they are much healthier than meat! If you're not familiar with cooking the raw version of these ingredients, then buy canned versions if you try and buy low sodium versions. They are great as a side or even as an addition to a healthy salad or taco.

Examples) lentils, chickpeas, beans (pinto, kidney, black, white), hummus

> Nuts and Seeds: Another category that is often overlooked, these are perfect snacks packed with healthy fats and protein. They contain omega 3 fatty acids as well as unsaturated fatty acids which are better for heart health. They are high in calories which is why you want to be aware of your intake and be sure you're not snacking mindlessly. Also, it's better if you choose unsalted or non-candy versions to ensure you're getting all the health benefits and none of the extra junk!

Examples) almonds, sunflower seeds, walnuts, hazelnuts, cashews, pumpkin seeds, pine nuts, chia seeds

Whole Grains: These healthy carbohydrates are allowed on the Mediterranean diet because of the essential vitamins, minerals, and fiber that they add to your diet. Fiber allows you to feel full for longer and keep your digestive system regular. Whole grains are much healthier than refined grains which means your blood sugar levels will stay stable. Incorporating just a side of this in your meals or as a component of your breakfast can help keep you energized.

Examples) couscous, whole grain pasta, quinoa, rice, pita bread, Ezekiel bread, oatmeal, barley

Extra Virgin Olive Oil: We talked about how extra virgin olive oil is such an important tenet of the Mediterranean diet. It may be a little more expensive to pay for the "extra virgin" label but just means it's the best quality of olive oil that is devoid of chemicals but still contains anti-inflammatory properties. If your olive oil has a label that says, "low fat," that means it's been treated with heat to change its properties. Be sure your bottle is opaque and made of dark glass or metal because exposure to light can ruin the oil. Keep it in a dark, cool place.

Examples) avocado oil, grapeseed oil, ghee, coconut oil is allowed as acceptable alternatives, but you should try and use extra virgin olive oil for all your needs

Fruit: The Mediterranean diet also encourages the moderate consumption of fresh fruit! Many diets prohibit it because of its natural sugar content or net carbs intake, but this diet urges you to use fruit as a natural dessert since you're forgoing refined sugar. The natural sugars found in fruit are much healthier for your body than anything artificially produced! You don't want to go overboard and eat too much a day but make fresh fruit an option to satisfy your sweet tooth or in a healthy smoothie.

Examples) bananas, apples, strawberries, melons, blueberries, dates, peaches, pears, oranges, and more!

Herbs and Spices: This is another tenet of Mediterranean cooking which allows you to season your food and add delicious flavor without simply relying on salt or fat in your food. If you don't have access to fresh herbs in a garden or can't seem to keep them fresh for long in your fridge, dried herbs are a great alternative. Be sure to browse your herb aisle at the grocery store to try new tastes and experiment with flavors that can add a lot of depth to your dishes. The calories are negligible, but the flavor is delicious!

10-Day Diet Meal Plan

Day	Breakfast	Lunch	Dinner
1	Breakfast Egg on Avocado	Favorite Pepper Soup	Easy Grilled Chicken Salad
2	Shakshuka	Parmesan and Chicken Veggie	Mediterranean Greens
3	Tiganites	Trout with Wilted Greens	Pear Salad with Creamy Yogurt Dressing
4	Cucumber Yogurt Salad	Delightful Pesto Pizza	Light and Fresh Arugula Salad

5	Veggie Wrap	Mediterranean Lamb Chops	Anchovy and Orange Salad
6	Scrambled Eggs	Tuna and Potato Salad	Blue Cheese and Arugula Salad
7	Creamy Paninis	Mushroom and Beef Risotto	Cucumber Salad Japanese Style
8	Dill and Tomato Frittata	Linguine Dredge in Tomato Clam Sauce	Delicious Bread Salad
9	Gingerbread Breakfast Quinoa	Oven Roasted Garlic Chicken Thigh	Simple Mixed Herb Salad
10	Mediterranean Pistachios and Fruits with Yogurt	Authentic Yogurt and Cucumber Salad	Asian Peanut Sauce Over Noodle Salad

Breakfast

1) Breakfast Egg on Avocado

Preparation time: 10 minutes

Cooking Time: 15 minutes

Servings: 6

Ingredients:

1 tsp garlic powder

1/2 tsp sea salt

1/4 cup Parmesan cheese (grated or shredded)

1/4 tsp black pepper

3 medium avocados (cut in half, pitted, skin on)

6 medium eggs

Directions for Cooking

Prepare muffin tins and preheat the oven to 350°F.

To ensure that the egg would fit inside the cavity of the avocado, lightly scrape off 1/3 of the meat.

Place avocado on muffin tin to ensure that it faces with the top up.

Evenly season each avocado with pepper, salt, and garlic powder.

Add one egg on each avocado cavity and garnish tops with cheese.

Pop in the oven and bake until the egg white is set, about 15 minutes.

Serve and enjoy.

Nutrition: Calories 252

Protein 14.0g

Carbs: 4.0g

Fat: 20.0g

2) Breakfast Egg-artichoke Casserole

Preparation time: 10 minutes

Cooking Time: 35 minutes

Servings: 8

Ingredients:

16 large eggs

14 ounce can artichoke hearts, drained

10-ounce box frozen chopped spinach, thawed and drained well

1 cup shredded white cheddar

1 garlic clove, minced

1 teaspoon salt

1/2 cup parmesan cheese

1/2 cup ricotta cheese

1/2 teaspoon dried thyme

1/2 teaspoon crushed red pepper

1/4 cup milk - 1/4 cup shaved onion

Directions: Lightly grease a 9x13-inch baking dish with cooking spray and preheat the oven to 350oF.

In a large mixing bowl, add eggs and milk. Mix thoroughly. With a paper towel, squeeze out the excess moisture from the spinach leaves and add to the bowl of eggs.

Into small pieces, break the artichoke hearts and separate the leaves. Add to the bowl of eggs.

Except for the ricotta cheese, add remaining ingredients in the bowl of eggs and mix thoroughly.

Pour egg mixture into the prepared dish.

Evenly add dollops of ricotta cheese on top of the eggs and then pop in the oven. Bake until eggs are set and doesn't jiggle when shook, about 35 minutes. Remove from the oven and evenly divide into suggested servings. Enjoy.

Nutrition: Calories 182

Protein 14.0g Carbs: 4.0g Fat: 20.0g

3) Brekky Egg-potato Hash

Preparation time: 10 minutes

Cooking Time: 25 minutes

Servings: 2

Ingredients:

1 zucchini, diced

1/2 cup chicken broth

½ pound cooked chicken

1 tablespoon olive oil

4 ounces shrimp

Salt and ground black pepper to taste

1 large sweet potato, diced

2 eggs

1/4 teaspoon cayenne pepper

2 teaspoons garlic powder

1 cup fresh spinach (optional)

Directions:

In a skillet, add the olive oil.

Fry the shrimp, cooked chicken and sweet potato for 2 minutes.

Add the cayenne pepper, garlic powder and salt, and toss for 4 minutes.

Add the zucchini and toss for another 3 minutes.

Whisk the eggs in a bowl and add to the skillet.

Season using salt and pepper. Cover with the lid.

Cook for 1 minute and add the chicken broth.

Cover and cook for another 8 minutes on high heat.

Add the spinach and toss for 2 more minutes.

Serve immediately.

Nutrition: Calories 190 Protein 14.0g

Carbs: 4.0g Fat: 20.0g

4) Dill and Tomato Frittata

Preparation time: 10 minutes

Cooking Time: 35 minutes

Servings: 6

Ingredients:

Pepper and salt to taste

1 tsp red pepper flakes

2 garlic cloves, minced

½ cup crumbled goat cheese – optional

2 tbsp fresh chives, chopped

2 tbsp fresh dill, chopped

4 tomatoes, diced

8 eggs, whisked

1 tsp coconut oil

Directions:

Grease a 9-inch round baking pan and preheat oven to 325oF.

In a large bowl, mix well all ingredients and pour into prepped pan.

Pop into the oven and bake until middle is cooked through around 30-35 minutes.

Remove from oven and garnish with more chives and dill.

Nutrition: Calories 124

Protein 14.0g

Carbs: 4.0g

Fat: 20.0g

5) Mediterranean Egg White Breakfast Sandwich

Preparation time: 10 minutes

Cooking Time: 25 minutes

Servings: 2

Ingredients:

2 teaspoons butter

Salt to taste

Pepper to taste

2 whole grain seeded ciabatta rolls, split, toasted

2 slices Swiss cheese or Muenster cheese

½ cup egg whites, beaten

2 teaspoon minced fresh herbs of your choice

2 tablespoons pesto

For roasted tomatoes:

2 tablespoons extra-virgin olive oil

20 ounces grape tomatoes, halved lengthwise

Kosher salt to taste

Coarsely ground pepper to taste

Directions:

Heat a nonstick pan over medium flame.

Toss half the butter and once it starts melting, add half the egg whites.

Sprinkle salt, pepper, and 1 teaspoon of herbs, and cook until the omelet is set. Flip sides and cook the other side for about 30 seconds. Place onto a plate.

Repeat steps 2-3 and make the other omelet.

Meanwhile make the roasted tomatoes as follows: Add tomatoes into a baking dish. Pour oil over it and toss well. Sprinkle with salt and pepper. Spread it evenly in the dish.

Roast in a preheated oven at 400° F for about 20 minutes or charred slightly.

Toast the rolls just before serving.

Spread pesto on the cut part of the rolls.

Place bottom halves of the rolls on individual serving plates. Place an omelet (fold the omelet to fit in) on each.

Place a slice of cheese on each. Cover with top half of the rolls and serve.

Nutrition: Calories 468

Protein 14.0g

Carbs: 4.0g

Fat: 20.0g

6) Mediterranean Breakfast Casserole

Preparation time: 10 minutes

Cooking Time: 35 minutes

Servings: 3

Ingredients

1 tablespoon olive oil

1 medium potato, peeled, diced

½ pound zucchini, sliced

1 small onion, chopped

2 medium sweet peppers, roasted, peeled

2 Portobello mushroom caps, chopped

1 cup chopped fresh spinach

3.5 ounces light ricotta cheese

3.5 ounces ricotta cheese

3 tablespoons part-skim milk mozzarella cheese, grated

2 tablespoons Pecorino Romano cheese, grated

6 grape tomatoes, sliced into thirds

1 cup egg whites

1 sourdough roll, cubed

Directions:

Place onion and potato in a baking dish. Drizzle a teaspoon of oil over it. Toss well and tilt the dish so it spreads evenly.

Bake in a preheated oven at 400° F for about 15 minutes. Transfer on to a baking tray.

Add zucchini into a bowl. Drizzle a teaspoon of oil over it. Toss well and transfer on to the baking tray (with potatoes). Bake for another 40 minutes or until golden brown.

Place a skillet over medium heat. Add 1 teaspoon oil. Once the oil heats, add mushrooms and sauté until soft. Remove from the pan and set aside.

Add 1 teaspoon oil to the same pan and place the pan overheat.

Add spinach and cook well, and then turn off the heat when the spinach wilts.

Add ricotta cheese and egg whites into a bowl and whisk well. Set aside.

Add zucchini, onion potato mixture, onion, sour dough roll cubes, and grape tomatoes into a baking dish and mix well.

Pour the ricotta mixture over it. Sprinkle mozzarella cheese and Pecorino Romano cheese.

Bake in a preheated oven at 400° F for 40-50 minutes or until the eggs are cooked as per your desire. Remove the baking dish from the oven and let it cool down for a couple of minutes. Cut it into slices and serve.

Nutrition: Calories 370.2

Fat 15.7 g

Carbohydrate 34.4 g

Fiber 4.6 g

Protein 25.8 g

7) Gingerbread Breakfast Quinoa Bake with Banana

Preparation time: 10 minutes

Cooking Time: 35 minutes

Servings: 4

Ingredients:

 3 small ripe bananas, mashed

 2 tablespoons pure maple syrup

 1 teaspoon raw vanilla extract

 ½ teaspoon ground cloves

 ¼ teaspoon salt or to taste

 1 ¼ cups unsweetened vanilla almond milk

 ¼ teaspoon ground allspice

 2 tablespoons molasses

 ½ teaspoon ground ginger

 ½ tablespoon ground cinnamon

 ½ cup quinoa, uncooked

2 tablespoons slivered almonds

Directions:

Add banana, maple syrup, vanilla, ginger, molasses, salt and all the spices into a casserole dish or baking dish. Mix until well incorporated.

Stir in the quinoa.

Add milk and whisk until well incorporated. Cover and chill overnight. Remove the dish from the refrigerator and give it a good stir. Cover the dish with foil.

Bake in a preheated oven at 400° F for 40-50 minutes or until dry and cooked through.

Set the oven to broil mode. Scatter the almonds on top. Press lightly to adhere.

Broil for three to four minutes or until almonds are golden brown on top. Remove the baking dish from the oven and let it cool for five to eight minutes. Cut it into four equal wedges and serve.

Nutrition: Calories 370.2 Fat 15.7 g

Carbohydrate 34.4 g Fiber 4.6 g

Protein 25.8 g

8) Egg Muffins with Vegetables and Feta Cheese

Preparation time: 10 minutes

Cooking time: 15 minutes

Servings: 6

Ingredients:

1 cup finely chopped baby spinach

½ cup chopped tomatoes

½ tablespoon chopped fresh oregano

4 eggs, well beaten

½ cup crumbled feta cheese

¼ cup finely chopped onions

¼ cup chopped, pitted Kalamata olives

1 teaspoon sunflower oil + extra to grease

½ cup cooked quinoa

Directions:

Grease a 6 counts muffin tin with some oil.

Heat a skillet over medium flame and add oil. Add onions and cook until they turn translucent.

Stir in the tomatoes and cook for a minute. Stir in the spinach and cook until it wilts. Remove from heat.

Add olives and oregano and mix well.

Add quinoa, salt, and feta cheese into the bowl of beaten eggs and whisk well.

Add the sautéed vegetables and mix well. Spoon into prepared muffin tins.

Bake in a preheated oven at 350° F for about 25 – 30 minutes or until it is done, and the top is light golden brown.

Remove from the oven and cool for a few minutes.

Run a knife around the edges of the muffin and loosen the muffins. Invert onto a plate and serve.

Nutrition: Calories 142.2 Fat 15.7 g

Carbohydrate 34.4 g Fiber 4.6 g

Protein 25.8 g

9) Mediterranean Breakfast Stir Fry (Melamen)

Preparation time: 10 minutes

Cooking time: 15 minutes

Servings: 8

Ingredients:

3 cups chopped onions

3 cups green bell peppers, chopped

4 large tomatoes, chopped

2 tablespoons extra-virgin olive oil

2 eggs, beaten

Pepper to taste

Salt to taste

Directions:

Heat a pan over a high flame. Add oil and then add bell pepper and sauté for a couple of minutes.

Reduce heat, cover and cook for two minutes.

Add onions and stir. Cover and cook for four to five minutes.

Add tomatoes, salt and pepper, stir and cover again. Cook until the tomatoes are soft.

Pour the beaten egg over the veggies in the pan. Do not stir at all. Let it simmer for 50 to 60 seconds.

Serve with pita bread, cucumbers, and low-fat feta cheese.

Nutrition: Calories 162

Fat 15.7 g

Carbohydrate 34.4 g

Fiber 4.6 g

Protein 25.8 g

10) Mediterranean Pistachios and Fruits with Yogurt

Preparation time: 10 minutes

Cooking time: 45 minutes

Servings: 6

Ingredients:

¾ cup pistachios, unsalted

¼ cup chopped dried apricots

1/8 teaspoon ground or grated nutmeg

1 teaspoon raw sugar

2 tablespoons dried pomegranate seeds or dried cranberries

1/8 teaspoon ground allspice

¼ teaspoon cinnamon

Greek yogurt to serve, as required

Directions:

Grease a rimmed baking sheet with cooking spray. Place pistachios on it.

Bake in a preheated oven at 350° F for about seven minutes or until nuts are toasted lightly. Remove from the oven and let it cool.

Transfer the pistachios into a bowl. Add rest of the ingredients except yogurt. Toss well.

Transfer into an airtight container. It can last for a week.

To serve: Serve required quantity of yogurt in serving bowls.

Add ¼ cup nut mixture in each bowl and serve.

Nutrition: Calories 162

Fat 15.7 g

Carbohydrate 34.4 g

Fiber 4.6 g

Protein 25.8 g

11) Mediterranean Eggs

Preparation time: 10 minutes

Cooking time: 25 minutes

Servings: 3

Ingredients:

1 medium onion, sliced

½ tablespoon extra-virgin olive oil

3 tablespoons firmly packed, julienne cut, sun-dried tomatoes

1.5 ounces crumbled feta cheese

Chopped parsley, to garnish

½ tablespoon butter

2 small cloves garlic, minced

3 large eggs

Kosher salt to taste

Freshly ground pepper to taste

Crusty ciabatta rolls, to serve

Directions:

Place a skillet (preferably cast iron) over medium-low heat. Add butter and oil. When the butter melts, stir in the onions and cook until brown. It can take at least 30 minutes. Stir occasionally.

Stir in sun-dried tomatoes and garlic and cook until aromatic. Spread it evenly. Crack eggs at different spots on top. Scatter feta cheese.

Sprinkle salt and pepper to taste.

Cover and cook until the eggs are cooked. Do not uncover for at least five minutes. Garnish with parsley. Serve over ciabatta rolls.

Nutrition: Calories 162 Fat 15.7 g Carbohydrate 34.4 g Fiber 4.6 g Protein 25.8 g

12) Shakshuka

Preparation time: 10 minutes

Cooking time: 15 minutes

Servings: 6

Ingredients:

2 medium onions, chopped

3 cloves garlic, sliced

3 red bell peppers, chopped

½ teaspoon sugar

6 eggs

3 tablespoons olive oil

½ teaspoon spicy harissa peppers

Salt to taste

Pepper to taste

1 ½ cans (15 ounces each) diced tomatoes

Directions:

Place a heavy bottomed skillet over medium heat. Add oil and let it heat.

Stir in the onions and cook until onions are tender. Then add the bell peppers and toss for two minutes.

Stir in the garlic and cook for a couple of minutes until aromatic.

Stir in the tomatoes, harissa peppers, salt, pepper, and sugar. Cook for about five to six minutes.

Make six holes in the mixture and crack an egg in each.

Cover with a lid and cook until the eggs are cooked.

Nutrition: Calories 162

Fat 15.7 g

Carbohydrate 34.4 g

Fiber 4.6 g

Protein 25.8 g

13) Veggie wrap

Preparation Time: 5 minutes

Cooking Time: 30 minutes

Servings: 6

Ingredients:

Tbsp Olive oil

¼ Tbsp dried crumbled rosemary

7 oz Chickpeas

¾ Tbsps. Oregano, dried and crumbled

¼ Tbsp. salt

¾ Tbsp. of dried thyme

1 Tbsp. of grounded pepper

2 medium-sized tomatoes

2 cucumbers, sliced

2 sliced onions

2 bell peppers, green

2 medium-sized zucchinis

6 flat wheat bread (whole) (8-10inches)

Directions:

Sprinkle the olive oil inside the non-stick pan. It serves as a spray.

Add the bell pepper tomatoes, onions, zucchini to the oil.

Sprinkle the thyme, dried rosemary, and oregano into the mixture and allow it to roast for about 15 minutes at 425°F.

Now add the chickpeas, cumin, then add the salt and pepper to taste.

Cook until it is tender. It will be ready in another 15 minutes.

Fill the bread with the veggie mix, roll it up, and serve. Add alfalfa sprouts if desired.

Nutrition:

Calories: 235 kcal

Carbs: 32g

Fat: 8g

Protein: 7g.

14) Tiganites

Preparation Time: 5 minutes

Cooking Time: 5 minutes

Servings: 4

Ingredients:

¼ cup honey/ petimezi

2 Tbsp. sugar

¾ tsp salt

2 large-sized eggs

¼ cup of vegetable oil

4 Tbsp of butter (unsalted)

2 cups of flour (all-purpose)

2 tsp baking powder

2 cups milk, whole

Directions:

In a bowl, mix the milk, egg, and oil together.

In another bowl, mix the flour, baking powder, sugar, and salt.

Combine the ingredients in both bowls together and mix thoroughly

In a large pan on medium heat, add 2 Tbsps. of butter and heat for about 30 seconds.

Pour ¼ cup of the mixed ingredients into the pan. Fry for about 2 minutes, and when it starts showing bubbles, flip it to the other side and fry again for another 2 minutes.

It is ready to be served. Serve with honey and leftover butter.

Nutrition:

Calories: 311 kcal

Carbs: 41g

Fat: 15g

Protein: 3g.

15) Greek Olive and Feta Cheese Pasta

Preparation Time: 90 minutes

Cooking Time: 15 minutes

Servings: 4

Ingredients:

2 cloves of finely minced fresh garlic

2 large tomatoes, seeded and diced

3 oz feta cheese, crumbled

½ diced red bell pepper

10 small-sized Greek olives, coarsely chopped and pitted

½ diced yellow bell pepper

¼ cup basil leaves, coarsely chopped

1 Tbsp Olive oil

¼ tsp hot pepper, finely chopped

4 ½ oz of ziti pasta

Directions:

Cook pasta to a desirable point, drain it, sprinkle with olive oil, and set aside.

In a large bowl, mix olives, feta cheese, basil, garlic, and hot pepper. Leave for 30 minutes.

To the same bowl, add the cooked pasta, the bell peppers, and toss. Refrigerate for up to an hour. Toss again, then serve chilled.

Nutrition:

Calories: 235 kcal

Carbs: 27g

Fat: 10g

Protein: 7g.

16) Tomatoes Stuffed with Goat Cheese

Preparation Time: 15 minutes

Cooking Time: 0 minutes

Servings: 2

Ingredients:

1 tsp. Extra Virgin Olive oil

Parsley, freshly chopped

3 oz feta cheese

7 Arugula leaves

Salt, to taste

Freshly grounded pepper, to taste

¼ tsp balsamic vinegar

1 red onion, thinly sliced

2 medium-sized ripe tomatoes

Directions:

Put 3-4 arugula leaves at the center of the two salad plates.

Slice ¼ inches off the top of each tomato. Core ½ inch off the center of each tomato.

Fill the space in the tomatoes with feta cheese, salt, and pepper to desired taste.

Drizzle each tomato with olive oil and balsamic vinegar

Garnish the top with slices of red onion and parsley. It is done.

Nutrition:

Calories: 142 kcal

Carbs: 7g

Fat: 13g

Protein: 7g.

17) Cucumber Yogurt Salad

Preparation Time: 10 minutes

Cooking Time: 0 minutes

Servings: 4

Ingredients:

2 peeled and diced English cucumbers

1 ½ Tbsps. fresh garlic, crushed

pinch of Salt

2 tsp. dried mint

1/8 Tbsp. fresh dill, already minced

1-quart low-fat yogurt, plain

Directions:

In a small bowl, mix the dill, garlic, and salt.

Pour the yogurt in and mix well.

Add cucumber, mint and stir well

Put inside the refrigerator to chill, then serve.

Nutrition: Calories: 167 kcal

Carbs: 21g Fat: 4g Protein: 13g.

18) Savory Greek White Fava Bean Salad

Preparation Time: 24 hours

Cooking Time: 60 minutes

Servings: 4

Ingredients:

3 Tbsp. olive-oil

1 onion, small and finely chopped

Salt

4 ½ Tbsp red wine vinegar

2-3 sage leaves, fresh

3 Tbsp lemon juice, freshly squeezed

Freshly grounded pepper

1 celery stalk, fresh and chopped

1 ¼ cup dried fava beans, white

½ Tbsp. of oregano, dried

2 cloves of finely minced garlic.

Directions:

Beans should be soaked in a lot of water overnight

The next morning drain the beans and make sure to rinse it with fresh water.

Put drained beans into another pot of fresh water, add sage, cover the pot, and allow it to cook for about 45 minutes.

Add salt.

Cook for another 15 minutes to allow beans to become soft.

Drain the beans, then add lemon juice, olive oil, onion, garlic, oregano, celery, and vinegar. Add pepper to desired taste.

Refrigerate for an hour before serving.

Nutrition:

Calories: 253 kcal

Carbs: 28g

Fat: 11g

Protein: 12g

19) Tangy Orange Roasted Asparagus Salad

Preparation Time: 24 hours

Cooking Time: 60 minutes

Servings: 4

Ingredients:

2 cloves of minced garlic

1 tsp. of basil leaf

Salt

6 cups of romaine lettuce

1 pound of fresh asparagus

20) Romano cheese preferably grated

4 tsp of orange juice

1 Tbsp. of lime juice

4 tsp of olive oil

Ground pepper

3 tsp. of toasted pine nuts

Directions:

Mix asparagus and 2 tsp of olive oil, salt to desired taste

Put already mixed asparagus in the oven, roast for 10 minutes until it is tender crispy.

In another bowl, mix garlic, orange juice, 2 tsp of olive oil, lime juice, and include salt and pepper to desired taste.

When it ready, add lettuce to the salad, put asparagus on top of it, and add pine nuts with basil. Add Romano cheese if desired.

Nutrition:

Calories: 253 kcal

Carbs: 28g

Fat: 11g

Protein: 12g

21) Mediterranean Mixed Greens

Preparation Time: 5 minutes

Cooking Time: 0 minutes

Servings: 5

Ingredients:

¼ cup of chopped walnuts

Ground pepper, to taste

6 cups mixed greens

¼ cup of dried cranberries

1 red onion

20 cherry tomatoes

Directions:

In a big bowl, mix the onion, walnuts, tomatoes, cranberries, and green

Stir thoroughly. Serve

Nutrition: Calories: 140 kcal

Carbs: 6g Fat: 13g

Protein: 2.5g

22) Creamy Paninis

Preparation Time: 10 minutes

Cooking Time: 5 minutes

Servings: 4

Ingredients:

1 zucchini mostly thinly sliced

½ cup of mayonnaise with olive oil

2 Tbsps. of black olives

¼ cup of basil leaves

7 oz of roasted red pepper

8 slices of wheat bread

4 slices bacon

4 slices of provolone cheese

Directions:

Inside a bowl, mix the mayonnaise, basil, and olives. Spread the mayonnaise mixture on the bread and place 4 slices of provolone and bacon, 1 slice zucchini and sprinkle the pepper all over. Place another slice of bread on top of it and put mayonnaise on it.

Butter the non-stick pan, then place the bread in and cook for about 4 minutes before you flip it to the other side.

Keep on heat until the sandwich is brown, and the cheese is already melted.

Serve.

Nutrition:

Calories: 553

Total Fat: 38.7g

Cholesterol: 50mg

Carbs: 28.1g

Fiber: 4.8g

Sugars: 6g

Protein: 22.3

23) Scrambled eggs

Preparation Time: 10 minutes

Cooking Time: 15 minutes

Servings: 2

Ingredients:

3 eggs

½ Tbsps. of olive oil

Salt

½ cup of ground beef

Pepper

½ Tbsp. of garlic powder

Directions:

Put the pan on medium heat

Drizzle olive oil in the pan and heat, add ground beef and let it cook for about 10 minutes

Add sauté and garlic and leave for 2 minutes

In another bowl, break the egg and beat it until its frothy, add salt and pepper

Put the already frothy egg inside the pan containing beef and oil. Wait till it is cooked. Serve with bread.

Nutrition:

Calories: 253 kcal

Carbs: 28g

Fat: 11g

Protein: 12g

Lunch

24) Favorite Pepper Soup

Preparation Time: 5 minutes

Cooking Time: 30 minutes

Serving: 6

Ingredients

1-pound lean ground beef
1 onion, chopped
1 large green pepper, chopped
2 garlic cloves, minced
1 large tomato, chopped
2 tablespoons tomato paste
2 tablespoons all-purpose flour
¼ cup uncooked rice
2 tablespoons fresh parsley, chopped
4 cups beef broth
2 tablespoons olive oil
Salt and pepper as needed

Direction:

Take a large-sized pot and place it over medium heat.

Add oil and allow the oil to heat up.

Add flour and keep whisking until you have a thick paste.

Keep whisking for 3-4 minutes more while it bubbles and begins to thin.

Add chopped onion and sauté for 3-4 minutes.

Stir in tomato paste and beef.

Take a wooden spoon and stir to break the ground beef.

Cook for 5 minutes.

Add garlic, pepper and chopped tomatoes.

Mix well and combine.

Add broth and bring the mix to a light boil, reduce the heat to low and simmer for 30 minutes.

Add rice, parsley and cook for 15 minutes.

Once it has a nice soup-like consistency, serve with garnish of parsley.

Enjoy!

Nutrition:

Calories: 162

Fat: 3g

Carbohydrates: 12g

Protein: 21g

25) The Mediterranean Tomato Soup

Preparation Time: 5 minutes

Cooking Time: 25 minutes

Serving: 6

Ingredients

4 tablespoons olive oil
2 medium yellow onion, thinly sliced
1 teaspoon salt
2 teaspoons curry powder
1 teaspoon red curry powder
1 teaspoon ground coriander
1 teaspoon ground cumin
1 can (15 ounces) Roma tomatoes, diced
1 can (28 ounce) plum tomatoes, diced
5 ½ cups water
1 can (14 ounces) coconut milk
Coconut brown rice, lemon wedges, fresh thyme, etc. as extra mix-ins

Direction:

Take a medium-sized pan and add oil.

Place it over medium heat and allow it to heat up.

Add onions and salt and cook for about 10-12 minutes until browned.

Stir in curry powder, coriander, red pepper flakes, cumin and cook for 30 seconds.

Make sure to keep stirring it well.

Add tomatoes alongside the juice and 5 ½ cups of water (or broth if you prefer).

Simmer the mixture for 15 minutes.

Take an immersion blender and puree the mixture until a soupy consistency is achieved.

Enjoy as it is or add some extra add-ins for a more flavorful experience.

Nutrition:

Calories: 74
Fat: 0.7g
Carbohydrates: 16g
Protein: 2g

26) Authentic Yogurt and Cucumber Salad

Preparation Time: 10 minutes

Cooking Time: 0

Serving: 4

Ingredients

5-6 small cucumbers, peeled and diced
1 (8 ounces) container plain Greek yogurt
2 garlic cloves, minced
1 tablespoon fresh mint, minced
1 teaspoon dried oregano
Sea salt and fresh black pepper

Direction:

Take a large bowl and add cucumbers, garlic, yogurt, mint, and oregano.

Season with salt and pepper.

Refrigerate the salad for 1 hour and serve.

Enjoy!

Nutrition:

Calories: 74
Fat: 0.7g
Carbohydrates: 16g
Protein: 2g

27) Delightful Pesto Pizza

Preparation Time: 25 minutes

Cooking Time: 20 minutes

Serving: 4

Ingredients

1 (10 inch) pizza crust, homemade/premade
½ cup sun-dried tomato pesto
1 cup button mushrooms, sliced
1 red bell pepper, chopped
1 cup zucchini, sliced
12 cup red onion, thinly sliced
½ cup black olives, sliced
½ cup Parmesan cheese, grated

Direction:

Pre-heat your oven to 400 degrees Fahrenheit.

Line a baking sheet with parchment paper and keep it on the side.

Dust the work surface with flour and roll our pizza dough to a 10-inch circle.

Transfer dough to baking sheet.

Spread pesto over dough (leaving 1 inch from edge).

Arrange mushrooms, red bell pepper, zucchini, onion and olives on pizza.

Top with cheese.

Bake for 20 minutes until golden and crispy.

Nutrition:

Calories: 210
Fat: 9g
Carbohydrates: 25g
Protein: 9g

28) Linguine Dredged in Tomato Clam Sauce

Preparation Time: 10 minutes

Cooking Time: 10 minutes

Serving: 4

Ingredients

1-pound linguine
Salt and black pepper as needed
1 teaspoon extra virgin olive oil
1 tablespoon garlic, minced
1 teaspoon fresh thyme, chopped
½ teaspoon red pepper flakes
1 can (15 ounces) sodium-free tomatoes, diced and drained
1 can (15 ounce) can whole baby clams, with juice

Direction:

Cook the linguine accordingly.

While linguine cooks, heat olive oil in a large skillet over medium heat.

Add garlic, thyme, red pepper flakes and sauté for 3 minutes.

Stir in tomatoes and clams.

Bring sauce to boil and lower heat to low.

Simmer for 5 minutes.

Season with salt and pepper.

Drain cooked pasta and toss with sauce.

Garnish with parsley and serve.

Enjoy!

Nutrition:

Calories: 394
Fat: 5g
Carbohydrates: 66g
Protein: 23g

29) Wild Mushrooms and Pork Chops

Preparation Time: 10 minutes

Cooking Time: 25 minutes

Serving: 4

Ingredients

4 (5 ounce) bone-in-center pork chops
¼ teaspoon sea salt
¼ teaspoon freshly ground black pepper
1 tablespoon extra-virgin olive oil
1 sweet onion, chopped
2 teaspoons garlic, minced
1-pound mixed wild mushrooms, sliced
1 teaspoon fresh thyme, chopped
½ cup sodium free chicken stock

Direction:

Pat pork chops dry with kitchen towel and season with salt and pepper.

Take a large skillet and place it over medium-high heat.

Add olive oil and heat it up.

Add pork chops and cook for 6 minutes, brown both sides.

Transfer meat to platter and keep aside.

Add onion and garlic and sauté for 3 minutes.

Stir in mushrooms and thyme and sauté for 6 minutes until the mushrooms are caramelized.

Return pork chops to the skillet and pour chicken stock.

Cover and bring liquid to boil.

Reduce heat to low and simmer for 10 minutes.

Serve and enjoy!

Nutrition:

Calories: 308
Fat: 17g
Carbohydrates: 7g
Protein: 33g

30) Mediterranean Lamb Chops

Preparation Time: 10 minutes

Cooking Time: 10 minutes

Serving: 4

Ingredients

4 lamb shoulder chops, 8 ounce each
2 tablespoons Dijon mustard
2 tablespoons Balsamic vinegar
1 tablespoon garlic, chopped
½ cup olive oil
2 tablespoons shredded fresh basil

Direction:

Pat your lamb chop dry using kitchen towel and arrange them on a shallow glass baking dish.

Take a bowl and whisk in Dijon mustard, balsamic vinegar, garlic, pepper and mix well.

Whisk in the oil very slowly into the marinade until the mixture is smooth.

Stir in basil.

Pour the marinade over the lamb chops and stir to coat both sides well.

Cover the chops and allow them to marinate for 1-4 hours (chilled).

Take the chops out and leave them for 30 minutes to allow the temperature to reach normal level.

Pre-heat your grill to medium heat and add oil to the grate.

Grill the lamb chops for 5-10 minutes per side until both sides are browned.

Once the center of the chop reads 145-degree Fahrenheit, the chops are ready, serve and enjoy!

Nutrition:

Calories: 521
Fat: 45g
Carbohydrates: 3.5g
Protein: 22g

31) Mushroom and Beef Risotto

Serving: 4

Preparation Time: 5 minutes

Cooking Time: 10 minutes

Ingredients

2 cups low-sodium beef stock
2 cups water
2 tablespoon olive oil
½ cup scallions, chopped
1 cup Arborio rice
¼ cup dry white wine
1 cup roast beef, thinly stripped
1 cup button mushrooms
½ cup canned cream of mushroom
Salt and pepper as needed
Oregano, chopped
Parsley, chopped

Direction:

Take a stock pot and put it over medium heat.

Add water with beef stock in it.

Bring the mixture to a boil and remove the heat.

Take another heavy-bottomed saucepan and put it over medium heat.

Add in the scallions and stir fry them for 1 minute.

Add in the rice then and cook it for at least 2 minutes, occasionally stirring it to ensure that it is finely coated with oil.

In the rice mixture, keep adding your beef stock ½ a cup at a time, making sure to stir it often.

Once all the stock has been added, cook the rice for another 2 minutes.

During the last 5 minutes of your cooking, make sure to add the beef, cream of mushroom, while stirring it nicely.

Transfer the whole mix to a serving dish.

Garnish with some chopped up parsley and oregano. Serve hot.

Nutrition: Calories: 378 Fat: 12g

Carbohydrates: 41g Protein: 23g

32) Broiled Mushrooms Burgers and Goat Cheese

Preparation Time: 15 minutes

Cooking Time: 5 minutes

Serving: 4

Ingredients

4 large Portobello mushroom caps
1 red onion, cut into ¼ inch thick slices
2 tablespoons extra virgin olive oil
2 tablespoons balsamic vinegar
Pinch of salt
¼ cup goat cheese
¼ cup sun-dried tomatoes, chopped
4 ciabatta buns
1 cup kale, shredded

Direction:

Pre-heat your oven to broil.

Take a large bowl and add mushrooms caps, onion slices, olive oil, balsamic vinegar and salt.

Mix well.

Place mushroom caps (bottom side up) and onion slices on your baking sheet.

Take a small bowl and stir in goat cheese and sun-dried tomatoes.

Toast the buns under the broiler for 30 seconds until golden.

Spread the goat cheese mix on top of each bun.

Place mushroom cap and onion slice on each bun bottom and cover with shredded kale.

Put everything together and serve.

Enjoy!

Nutrition:

Calories: 327
Fat: 11g
Carbohydrates: 49g
Protein: 11g

33) Tuna and Potato Salad

Preparation Time: 10 minutes

Cooking Time: 0

Serving: 4

Ingredients

1-pound baby potatoes, scrubbed, boiled
1 cup tuna chunks, drained
1 cup cherry tomatoes, halved
1 cup medium onion, thinly sliced
8 pitted black olives
2 medium hard-boiled eggs, sliced
1 head Romaine lettuce
Honey lemon mustard dressing
¼ cup olive oil
2 tablespoons lemon juice
1 tablespoon Dijon mustard
1 teaspoon dill weed, chopped
Salt as needed
Pepper as needed

Direction:

Take a small glass bowl and mix in your olive oil, honey, lemon juice, Dijon mustard and dill.

Season the mix with pepper and salt.

Add in the tuna, baby potatoes, cherry tomatoes, red onion, green beans, black olives and toss. everything nicely.

Arrange your lettuce leaves on a beautiful serving dish to make the base of your salad.

Top them with your salad mixture and place the egg slices.

Drizzle it with the previously prepared Salad Dressing.

Serve hot.

Nutrition:

Calories: 406
Fat: 22g
Carbohydrates: 28g
Protein: 26g

34) Parmesan and Chicken Veggie

Preparation Time: 5 minutes

Cooking Time: 0 minute

Serving: 4

Ingredients

3 cups cooked shell pasta
2 cups baby spinach, torn
1 cup roasted cherry tomatoes, halved
8 ounces roasted chicken breast, cut into strips
¼ cup Parmesan cheese, grated
Lemon vinaigrette dressing
1/3 cup extra-virgin olive oil
2 tablespoons lemon juice
1 teaspoon lemon zest, finely grated
½ teaspoon dried rosemary
Salt and pepper as needed

Direction:

Take a glass bowl and whisk in oil, zest, lemon juice and rosemary.

Keep the mixture to the side.

Take another large bowl and add spinach, pasta, cherry tomatoes, chicken and drizzle the dressing on top.

Season with salt and pepper.

Toss until coated well.

Divide the salad amongst serving plates and sprinkle cheese on top.

Serve and enjoy!

Nutrition:

Calories: 398

Fat: 23g

Carbohydrates: 24g

Protein: 24g

35) Mushroom and Pork Chops

Preparation Time: 10 minutes

Cooking Time: 25 minutes

Serving: 4

Ingredients

4 (5 ounce) bone-in-center pork chops
¼ teaspoon sea salt
¼ teaspoon freshly ground black pepper
1 tablespoon extra-virgin olive oil
1 sweet onion, chopped
2 teaspoons garlic, minced
1-pound mixed wild mushrooms, sliced
1 teaspoon fresh thyme, chopped
½ cup sodium free chicken stock

Direction:

Pat pork chops dry with kitchen towel and season with salt and pepper.

Take a large skillet and place it over medium-high heat.

Add olive oil and heat it up.

Add pork chops and cook for 6 minutes, brown both sides.

Transfer meat to platter and keep it aside.

Add onion and garlic and sauté for 3 minutes.

Stir in mushrooms and thyme and sauté for 6 minutes until the mushrooms are caramelized.

Return pork chops to the skillet and pour chicken stock.

Cover and bring liquid to boil.

Reduce the heat to low and simmer for 10 minutes.

Serve and enjoy!

Nutrition:

Calories: 308
Fat: 17g
Carbohydrates: 7g
Protein: 33g

36) Oven Roasted Garlic Chicken Thigh

Preparation Time: 10 minutes

Cooking Time: 55 minutes

Serving: 4

Ingredients

8 chicken thighs
Salt and pepper as needed
1 tablespoon extra-virgin olive oil
6 cloves garlic, peeled and crushed
1 jar (10 ounce) roasted red peppers, drained and chopped
1 1/2 pounds potatoes, diced
2 cups cherry tomatoes, halved
1/3 cup capers, sliced
1 teaspoon dried Italian seasoning
1 tablespoon fresh basil

Direction:

Season chicken with kosher salt and black pepper.

Take a cast iron skillet over medium-high heat and heat up olive oil.

Sear the chicken on both sides.

Add remaining ingredients except basil and stir well.

Remove heat and place cast iron skillet in the oven.

Bake for 45 minutes at 400 degrees Fahrenheit until the internal temperature reaches 165 degrees Fahrenheit.

Serve and enjoy!

Nutrition:

Calories: 500
Fat: 23g
Carbohydrates: 37g
Protein: 35g

37) Trout with Wilted Greens

Preparation Time: 5 minutes

Cooking Time: 15 minutes

Serving: 4

Ingredients

2 teaspoons extra virgin olive oil
2 cups kale, chopped
2 cups Swiss chard, chopped
½ sweet onion, thinly sliced
4 (5 ounce) boneless skin-on trout fillets
Juice of 1 lemon
Sea salt
Freshly ground pepper
Zest of 1 lemon

Direction:

Pre-heat your oven to 375 degrees Fahrenheit.

Lightly grease a 9 by 13-inch baking dish with olive oil.

Arrange the kale, Swiss chard, onion in a dish.

Top greens with fish, skin side up and drizzle with olive oil and lemon juice.

Season fish with salt and pepper.

Bake for 15 minutes until fish flakes.

Sprinkle zest.

Serve and enjoy!

Nutrition:

Calories: 315
Fat: 14g
Carbohydrates: 6g
Protein: 39g

Salad

38) Easy Grilled Chicken Salad

Preparation Time: 10 minutes

Cooking time 20 minutes

Servings 4

Ingredients: Chicken fillets - 2

Extra virgin olive oil - 2 tbsp.

Dried basil - 1 tsp.   Oregano - 1 tsp.

Salt and pepper - to taste

Olive oil - 2 tbsp.

Arugula - 2 cups of leaves

Cherry tomatoes - 1 cup, halved

Green olives - 1 4 cup

Cucumber - 1, sliced

Lemon - 1, juiced

Directions: Mix all above Ingredients: (except chicken, salt, pepper, oregano, basil and olive oil) in a large salad bowl and set aside.

Season the chicken with salt, pepper, oregano and basil then drizzle it with olive oil.

Sprinkle oregano, basil, salt and pepper onto chicken fillets evenly and then drizzle olive oil over fillets.

Put chicken fillets into a skillet over medium heat and cook until browned and cooked through.

Cut chicken into strips or dice.

Add chicken to the other Ingredients: and stir together.

Season with salt and pepper to suit your taste. Salad is best when served fresh.

Nutrition: calories 340 fat 23

fiber 12 carbs 23 protein 25

39) Light and Fresh Arugula Salad

Preparation Time: 10 minutes

Cooking time 0 minutes

Servings: 3

Ingredients:

Brie cheese - 8 oz., crumbled

Balsamic vinegar - 2 tbsp.

Arugula leaves - 2 cups, rinsed

Extra virgin olive oil - 2 tbsp.

Quail eggs - 8, cooked and cut in half

Directions:

Mix all Ingredients: together in a large salad bowl.

The work is done, and this salad is ready to eat. Best if eaten right away.

Nutrition: calories 340 fat 23 fiber 12 carbs 23 protein 25

40) Mediterranean Greens

Preparation Time: 10 minutes

Cooking time 0 minutes

Servings: 2

Ingredients: Parsley - 1 2 cup, chopped

Baby spinach - 2 cups

Balsamic vinegar - 1 tbsp.

Celery stalks - 2, sliced

Arugula leaves - 2 cups

Cucumbers - 2, sliced

Cilantro - 1 4 cup, chopped

Lemon - 1, juiced

Salt and pepper - to taste

Directions: Mix all Ingredients: except salt and pepper, in a large salad bowl. Season with salt and pepper to suit your taste. This easy, fresh salad is ready to serve.

Nutrition: calories 340 fat 23 fiber 12 carbs 23 protein 25

41) Pear salad with creamy yogurt dressing

Preparation Time: 10 minutes

Cooking time 0 minutes

Servings: 3

Ingredients:

Arugula - 4 cups

Pears - 4, cored and sliced

Walnuts - 1 2 cup, chopped

Blue cheese - 2 oz., crumbled

Plain yogurt - 1 4 cup

Lemon juice - 1 tbsp.

Extra virgin olive oil - 2 tbsp.

Salt and pepper - to taste

Directions:

Using a jar or bottle, mix together lemon juice, yogurt, oil and salt and pepper to taste to make dressing, shaking well.

Now mix pears, blue cheese, sliced pears and walnuts in a separate, large salad bowl.

Lightly dress salad with yogurt mixture and eat immediately.

Nutrition: calories 340

fat 23

fiber 12

carbs 23

protein 25

42) Anchovy and Orange Salad

Preparation Time: 10 minutes

Cooking time 30 minutes

Servings: 2

Ingredients:

1 small red onion, sliced into thin rounds

1 tbsp fresh lemon juice

1/8 tsp pepper or more to taste

16 oil cure Kalamata olives

2 tsp finely minced fennel fronds for garnish

3 tbsp extra virgin olive oil

4 small oranges, preferably blood oranges

6 anchovy fillets

Directions:

With a paring knife, peel oranges including the membrane that surrounds it.

In a plate, slice oranges into thin circles and allow plate to catch the orange juices.

On serving plate, arrange orange slices on a layer.

Sprinkle oranges with onion, followed by olives and then anchovy fillets.

Drizzle with oil, lemon juice and orange juice.

Sprinkle with pepper.

Allow salad to stand for 30 minutes at room temperature to allow the flavors to develop.

To serve, garnish with fennel fronds and enjoy.

Nutrition: calories 133

fat 23

fiber 12

carbs 23

protein 25

43) Asian Peanut Sauce Over Noodle Salad

Preparation Time: 10 minutes

Cooking time 15 minutes

Servings: 3

Ingredients:

¼ cup sugar free peanut butter

¼ teaspoon cayenne pepper

½ cup filtered water

½ teaspoon kosher salt

1 tablespoon fish sauce (or coconut amines for vegan)

1 tablespoon granulated erythritol sweetener

1 tablespoon lime juice

1 tablespoon toasted sesame oil

1 tablespoon wheat-free soy sauce

1 teaspoon minced garlic

2 tablespoons minced ginger

Directions:

In a large salad bowl, combine all noodle salad ingredients and toss well to mix.

In a blender, mix all sauce ingredients and pulse until smooth and creamy.

Pour sauce over the salad and toss well to coat.

Evenly divide into four equal servings and enjoy.

Nutrition: calories 340

fat 23

fiber 12 carbs 23

protein 25

44) Blue Cheese and Arugula Salad

Preparation Time: 10 minutes

Cooking time 10 minutes

Servings: 2

Ingredients:

¼ cup crumbled blue cheese

1 tsp Dijon mustard

1-pint fresh figs, quartered

2 bags arugula

3 tbsp Balsamic Vinegar

3 tbsp olive oil

Pepper and salt to taste

Directions:

Whisk thoroughly together pepper, salt, olive oil, Dijon mustard, and balsamic vinegar to make the dressing. Set aside in the ref for at least 30 minutes to marinate and allow the spices to combine.

On four serving plates, evenly arrange arugula and top with blue cheese and figs.

Drizzle each plate of salad with 1 ½ tbsp of prepared dressing.

Serve and enjoy.

Nutrition: calories 340

fat 23

fiber 12

carbs 23

protein 25

45) Classic Greek Salad

Preparation Time: 10 minutes

Cooking time 15 minutes

Servings: 3

Ingredients:

¼ cup extra virgin olive oil, plus more for drizzling

¼ cup red wine vinegar

1 4-oz block Greek feta cheese packed in brine

1 cup Kalamata olives, halved and pitted

1 lemon, juiced and zested

1 small red onion, halved and thinly sliced

1 tsp dried oregano

1 tsp honey

14 small vine-ripened tomatoes, quartered

5 Persian cucumbers

Fresh oregano leaves for topping, optional

Pepper to taste Salt to taste

Directions:

In a bowl of ice water, soak red onions with 2 tbsp salt.

In a large bowl, whisk well ¼ tsp pepper, ½ tsp salt, dried oregano, honey, lemon zest, lemon juice, and vinegar. Slowly pour olive oil in a steady stream as you briskly whisk mixture. Continue whisking until emulsified.

Add olives and tomatoes, toss to coat with dressing.

Alternatingly peel cucumber leaving strips of skin on. Trim ends slice lengthwise and chop in ½-inch thick cubes. Add into bowl of tomatoes.

Drain onions and add into bowl of tomatoes. Toss well to coat and mix.

Drain feta and slice into four equal rectangles.

Divide Greek salad into serving plates, top each with oregano and feta.

To serve, season with pepper and drizzle with oil and enjoy.

Nutrition: calories 365

fat 23

fiber 12

carbs 23

protein 25

46) Cucumber Salad Japanese Style

Preparation Time: 10 minutes

Cooking time 15 minutes

Servings: 4

Ingredients:

1 ½ tsp minced fresh ginger root

1 tsp salt

1/3 cup rice vinegar

2 large cucumbers, ribbon cut

4 tsp white sugar

Directions:

Mix well ginger, salt, sugar and vinegar in a small bowl.

Add ribbon cut cucumbers and mix well.

Let stand for at least one hour in the ref before serving.

Nutrition: calories 340

fat 23

fiber 12 carbs 23 protein 25

47) Simple Mixed Herb Salad

Preparation time: 30 minutes

Cooking time: 35 minutes

Servings: 4

Ingredients:

tablespoons olive oil

1/3 cup tahini ½ cup raisins

4 tablespoons lemon juice

1 tablespoon water

¼ cup chives, chopped

¾ cup parsley, chopped

¼ cup cilantro, chopped

Salt and black pepper to taste

¼ cup fennel, chopped

¼ cup dill, chopped

¼ cup mint leaves, torn radishes, cut into matchsticks

¼ cup pistachios, toasted

¼ cup tarragon, chopped

1 tablespoon sesame seed, toasted

Directions:

Put raisins in a bowl, add warm water to cover, leave aside for 30 minutes, drain and put in a bowl.

In a small bowl, mix tahini with 3 tablespoons lemon juice, 3 tablespoons oil, salt, pepper and 1 tablespoon water and whisk well.

Arrange this on serving plates and leave them aside for now.

In a salad bowl, mix parsley with cilantro, chives, fennel, mint, dill, tarragon, remaining oil, the rest of the lemon juice, salt and pepper and toss to coat.

Nutrition: calories 232

fat 23

fiber 12

carbs 23

protein 25

48) Delicious Bread Salad

Preparation time: 10 minutes

Cooking time: 7 minutes

Servings: 4

Ingredients:

1 shallot, chopped

¼ cup lemon juice

5 ounces bread, cubed

½ teaspoon sugar tablespoons olive oil

Salt and black pepper to the taste

15 ounces canned chickpeas, drained

1/3 cup mint, chopped ounces cherry tomatoes cut in halves ounces feta cheese, crumbled

6 ounces snap peas, cut in quarters

3 ounces baby arugula

Directions:

Arrange the bread cubes in the oven at 350 degrees F, bake for 7 minutes and set aside to cool down.

In a bowl, mix sugar with shallot, lemon juice, salt and pepper, stir and set aside for 10 minutes.

Add the oil and mint and whisk well. In a salad bowl, mix tomatoes with snap peas, chickpeas and the vinaigrette and toss to coat.

Add arugula, feta cheese, bread cubes, toss again to coat and serve right away.

Nutrition: calories 340

fat 23

fiber 12

carbs 23

protein 25

Fish

49) Fish and Orzo

Preparation time: 10 minutes

Cooking time: 35 minutes

Servings: 4

Ingredients:

1 teaspoon garlic, minced
1 teaspoon red pepper, crushed
2 shallots, chopped
1 tablespoon olive oil
1 teaspoon anchovy paste
1 tablespoon oregano, chopped
2 tablespoons black olives, pitted and chopped
2 tablespoons capers, drained
15 ounces canned tomatoes, crushed
A pinch of salt and black pepper
4 cod fillets, boneless
1-ounce feta cheese, crumbled
1 tablespoons parsley, chopped
3 cups chicken stock
1 cup orzo pasta
Zest of 1 lemon, grated

Directions:

Heat up a pan with the oil over medium heat, add the garlic, red pepper and the shallots and sauté for 5 minutes.

Add the anchovy paste, oregano, black olives, capers, tomatoes, salt and pepper, stir and cook for 5 minutes more.

Add the cod fillets, sprinkle the cheese and the parsley on top, introduce in the oven and bake at 375 degrees F for 15 minutes more.

Meanwhile, put the stock in a pot, bring to a boil over medium heat, add the orzo and the lemon zest, bring to a simmer, cook for 10 minutes, fluff with a fork, and divide between plates.

Top each serving with the fish mix and serve.

Nutrition: calories 402

fat 23

fiber 12

carbs 23

protein 25

50) Baked Sea Bass

Preparation time: 10 minutes

Cooking time: 12 minutes

Servings: 4

Ingredients:

4 sea bass fillets, boneless
Sal and black pepper to the taste
2 cups potato chips, crushed
1 tablespoon mayonnaise

Directions:

Season the fish fillets with salt and pepper, brush with the mayonnaise and dredge each in the potato chips. Arrange the fillets on a baking sheet lined with parchment paper and bake at 400 degrees F for 12 minutes. Divide the fish between plates and serve with a side salad.

Nutrition: calories 402

fat 23

fiber 12

carbs 23

protein 25

51) Fish and Tomato Sauce

Preparation time: 10 minutes

Cooking time: 30 minutes

Servings: 4

Ingredients:

4 cod fillets, boneless
2 garlic cloves, minced
2 cups cherry tomatoes, halved
1 cup chicken stock
A pinch of salt and black pepper
¼ cup basil, chopped

Directions:

Put the tomatoes, garlic, salt and pepper in a pan, heat up over medium heat and cook for 5 minutes. Add the fish and the rest of the ingredients, bring to a simmer, cover the pan and cook for 25 minutes. Divide the mix between plates and serve.

Nutrition: calories 180

fat 23

fiber 12

carbs 23

protein 25

52) Halibut and Quinoa Mix

Preparation time: 10 minutes

Cooking time: 12 minutes

Servings: 4

Ingredients:

4 halibut fillets, boneless

2 tablespoons olive oil

1 teaspoon rosemary, dried

2 teaspoons cumin, ground

1 tablespoons coriander, ground

2 teaspoons cinnamon powder

2 teaspoons oregano, dried

A pinch of salt and black pepper

2 cups quinoa, cooked

1 cup cherry tomatoes, halved

1 avocado, peeled, pitted and sliced

1 cucumber, cubed

½ cup black olives, pitted and sliced

Juice of 1 lemon

Directions:

In a bowl, combine the fish with the rosemary, cumin, coriander, cinnamon, oregano, salt and pepper and toss.

Heat up a pan with the oil over medium heat, add the fish, and sear for 2 minutes on each side.

Introduce the pan in the oven and bake the fish at 425 degrees F for 7 minutes.

Meanwhile, in a bowl, mix the quinoa with the remaining

ingredients, toss and divide between plates.

Add the fish next to the quinoa mix and serve right away.

Nutrition: calories 402

fat 23

fiber 12

carbs 23

protein 25

53) Lemon and Dates Barramundi

Preparation time: 10 minutes

Cooking time: 12 minutes

Servings: 2

Ingredients:

2 barramundi fillets, boneless
1 shallot, sliced
4 lemon slices
Juice of ½ lemon
Zest of 1 lemon, grated
2 tablespoons olive oil
6 ounces baby spinach
¼ cup almonds, chopped
4 dates, pitted and chopped
¼ cup parsley, chopped
Salt and black pepper to the taste

Directions:

Season the fish with salt and pepper and arrange on 2 parchment paper pieces.

Top the fish with the lemon slices, drizzle the lemon juice, and then top with the other ingredients except the oil.

Drizzle 1 tablespoon oil over each fish mix, wrap the parchment paper around the fish shaping to packets and arrange them on a baking sheet.

Bake at 400 degrees F for 12 minutes, cool the mix a bit, unfold, divide everything between plates and serve.

Nutrition: calories 232

fat 23

fiber 12

carbs 23

protein 25

54) Fish Cakes

Preparation time: 10 minutes

Cooking time: 10 minutes

Servings: 6

Ingredients:

20 ounces canned sardines, drained and mashed well
2 garlic cloves, minced
2 tablespoons dill, chopped
1 yellow onion, chopped
1 cup panko breadcrumbs
1 egg, whisked
A pinch of salt and black pepper
2 tablespoons lemon juice
5 tablespoons olive oil

Directions:

In a bowl, combine the sardines with the garlic, dill and the rest of the ingredients except the oil, stir well and shape medium cakes out of this mix.

Heat up a pan with the oil over medium-high heat, add the fish cakes, cook for 5 minutes on each side.

Serve the cakes with a side salad.

Nutrition: calories 402

fat 23

fiber 12

carbs 23

protein 25

55) Catfish Fillets and Rice

Preparation time: 10 minutes

Cooking time: 55 minutes

Servings: 2

Ingredients:

2 catfish fillets, boneless
2 tablespoons Italian seasoning
2 tablespoons olive oil

For the rice:

1 cup brown rice
2 tablespoons olive oil
1 and ½ cups water
½ cup green bell pepper, chopped
2 garlic cloves, minced
½ cup white onion, chopped

2 teaspoons Cajun seasoning

½ teaspoon garlic powder

Salt and black pepper to the taste

Directions:

Heat up a pot with 2 tablespoons oil over medium heat, add the onion, garlic, garlic powder, salt and pepper and sauté for 5 minutes.

Add the rice, water, bell pepper and the seasoning, bring to a simmer and cook over medium heat for 40 minutes.

Heat up a pan with 2 tablespoons oil over medium heat, add the fish and the Italian seasoning, and cook for 5 minutes on each side.

Divide the rice between plates, add the fish on top and serve.

Nutrition: calories 261

fat 23

fiber 12

carbs 23

protein 25

56) Halibut Pan

Preparation time: 10 minutes

Cooking time: 20 minutes

Servings: 4

Ingredients:

4 halibut fillets, boneless

1 red bell pepper, chopped

2 tablespoons olive oil

1 yellow onion, chopped

4 garlic cloves, minced

½ cup chicken stock

1 teaspoon basil, dried

½ cup cherry tomatoes, halved

1/3 cup kalamata olives, pitted and halved

Salt and black pepper to the taste

Directions:

Heat up a pan with the oil over medium heat, add the fish, cook for 5 minutes on each side and divide between plates.

Add the onion, bell pepper, garlic and tomatoes to the pan, stir and sauté for 3 minutes.

Add salt, pepper and the rest of the ingredients, toss, cook for 3 minutes more, divide next to the fish and serve.

Nutrition: calories 402

fat 23

fiber 12

carbs 23

protein 25

57) Baked Shrimp Mix

Preparation time: 10 minutes

Cooking time: 32 minutes

Servings: 4

Ingredients:

4 gold potatoes, peeled and sliced
2 fennel bulbs, trimmed and cut into wedges
2 shallots, chopped
2 garlic cloves, minced
3 tablespoons olive oil
½ cup kalamata olives, pitted and halved
2 pounds shrimp, peeled and deveined
1 teaspoon lemon zest, grated
2 teaspoons oregano, dried
4 ounces feta cheese, crumbled
2 tablespoons parsley, chopped

Directions:

In a roasting pan, combine the potatoes with 2 tablespoons oil, garlic and the rest of the ingredients except the shrimp, toss, introduce in the oven and bake at 450 degrees F for 25 minutes.

Add the shrimp, toss, bake for 7 minutes more, divide between plates and serve.

Nutrition: calories 341

fat 23

fiber 12

carbs 23

protein 25

58) Shrimp and Lemon Sauce

Preparation time: 10 minutes

Cooking time: 15 minutes

Servings: 4

Ingredients:

1-pound shrimp, peeled and deveined
1/3 cup lemon juice
4 egg yolks
2 tablespoons olive oil
1 cup chicken stock
Salt and black pepper to the taste
1 cup black olives, pitted and halved
1 tablespoon thyme, chopped

Directions:

In a bowl, mix the lemon juice with the egg yolks and whisk well.

Heat up a pan with the oil over medium heat, add the shrimp and cook for 2 minutes on each side and transfer to a plate.

Heat up a pan with the stock over medium heat, add some of this over the egg yolks and lemon juice mix and whisk well.

Add this over the rest of the stock, also add salt and pepper, whisk well and simmer for 2 minutes.

Add the shrimp and the rest of the ingredients, toss and serve right away.

Nutrition: calories 237

fat 23

fiber 12

carbs 23

protein 25

59) Shrimp and Beans Salad

Preparation time: 10 minutes

Cooking time: 4 minutes

Servings: 4

Ingredients:

1-pound shrimp, peeled and deveined

30 ounces canned cannellini beans, drained and rinsed
2 tablespoons olive oil
1 cup cherry tomatoes, halved
1 teaspoon lemon zest, grated
½ cup red onion, chopped
4 handfuls baby arugula
A pinch of salt and black pepper
For the dressing:

3 tablespoons red wine vinegar
2 garlic cloves, minced
½ cup olive oil

Directions:

Heat up a pan with 2 tablespoons oil over medium-high heat, add the shrimp and cook for 2 minutes on each side.
In a salad bowl, combine the shrimp with the beans and the rest of the ingredients except the ones for the dressing and toss. In a separate bowl, combine the vinegar with ½ cup oil and the garlic and whisk well. Pour over the salad, toss and serve right away.

Nutrition: calories 207, fat 12.3, fiber 6.6, carbs 15.4, protein 8.7

60) Pecan Salmon Fillets

Preparation time: 10 minutes

Cooking time: 15 minutes

Servings: 6

Ingredients:

3 tablespoons olive oil
3 tablespoons mustard
5 teaspoons honey
1 cup pecans, chopped
6 salmon fillets, boneless
1 tablespoon lemon juice
3 teaspoons parsley, chopped
Salt and pepper to the taste

Directions:

In a bowl, mix the oil with the mustard and honey and whisk well. Put the pecans and the parsley in another bowl.
Season the salmon fillets with salt and pepper, arrange them on a baking sheet lined with parchment paper, brush with the honey and mustard mix and top with the pecans mix.

Introduce in the oven at 400 degrees F, bake for 15 minutes, divide between plates, drizzle the lemon juice on top and serve.

Nutrition: calories 402

fat 23

fiber 12

carbs 23

protein 25

61) Salmon and Broccoli

Preparation time: 10 minutes

Cooking time: 20 minutes

Servings: 4

Ingredients:

2 tablespoons balsamic vinegar
1 broccoli head, florets separated
4 pieces salmon fillets, skinless
1 big red onion, roughly chopped
1 tablespoon olive oil
Sea salt and black pepper to the taste

Directions:

In a baking dish, combine the salmon with the broccoli and the rest of the ingredients, introduce in the oven and bake at 390 degrees F for 20 minutes.

Divide the mix between plates and serve.

Nutrition: calories 321

fat 23

fiber 12

carbs 23

protein 25

62) Salmon and Peach Pan

Preparation time: 10 minutes

Cooking time: 11 minutes

Servings: 4

Ingredients:

1 tablespoon balsamic vinegar
1 teaspoon thyme, chopped
1 tablespoon ginger, grated
2 tablespoons olive oil

Sea salt and black pepper to the taste

3 peaches, cut into medium wedges

4 salmon fillets, boneless

Directions:

Heat up a pan with the oil over medium-high heat, add the salmon and cook for 3 minutes on each side. Add the vinegar, the peaches and the rest of the ingredients, cook for 5 minutes more, divide everything between plates and serve.

Nutrition: calories 211

fat 23

fiber 12

carbs 23

protein 25

63) Tarragon Cod Fillets

Preparation time: 10 minutes

Cooking time: 12 minutes

Servings: 4

Ingredients:

4 cod fillets, boneless

¼ cup capers, drained

1 tablespoon tarragon, chopped

Sea salt and black pepper to the taste

2 tablespoons olive oil

2 tablespoons parsley, chopped

1 tablespoon olive oil

1 tablespoon lemon juice

Directions:

Heat up a pan with the oil over medium-high heat, add the fish and cook for 3 minutes on each side. Add the rest of the ingredients, cook everything for 7 minutes more, divide between plates and serve.

Nutrition: calories 162 fat 23

fiber 12 carbs 23 protein 25

64) Salmon and Radish Mix

Preparation time: 10 minutes

Cooking time: 15 minutes

Servings: 4

Ingredients:

2 tablespoons olive oil

1 tablespoon balsamic vinegar

1 and ½ cup chicken stock

4 salmon fillets, boneless

2 garlic cloves, minced

1 tablespoon ginger, grated

1 cup radishes, grated

¼ cup scallions, chopped

Directions:

Heat up a pan with the oil over medium-high heat, add the salmon, cook for 4 minutes on each side and divide between plates
Add the vinegar and the rest of the ingredients to the pan, toss gently, cook for 10 minutes, add over the salmon and serve.

Nutrition: calories 402

fat 23

fiber 12

carbs 23

protein 25

65) Smoked Salmon and Watercress Salad

Preparation time: 5 minutes

Cooking time: 0 minutes

Servings: 4

Ingredients:

2 bunches watercress

1-pound smoked salmon, skinless, boneless and flaked

2 teaspoons mustard

¼ cup lemon juice

½ cup Greek yogurt

Salt and black pepper to the taste

1 big cucumber, sliced

2 tablespoons chives, chopped

Directions:

In a salad bowl, combine the salmon with the watercress and the rest of the ingredients toss and serve right away.

Nutrition: calories 244

fat 23

fiber 12

carbs 23

protein 25

66) Salmon and Corn Salad

Preparation time: 5 minutes

Cooking time: 0 minutes

Servings: 4

Ingredients:

½ cup pecans, chopped
2 cups baby arugula
1 cup corn
¼ pound smoked salmon, skinless, boneless and cut into small chunks
2 tablespoons olive oil
2 tablespoon lemon juice
Sea salt and black pepper to the taste

Directions:

In a salad bowl, combine the salmon with the corn and the rest of the ingredients, toss and serve right away.

Nutrition: calories 402

fat 23

fiber 12 carbs 23 protein 25

67) Cod and Mushrooms Mix

Preparation time: 10 minutes

Cooking time: 25 minutes

Servings: 4

Ingredients:

2 cod fillets, boneless
4 tablespoons olive oil
4 ounces mushrooms, sliced
Sea salt and black pepper to the taste
12 cherry tomatoes, halved
8 ounces lettuce leaves, torn
1 avocado, pitted, peeled and cubed
1 red chili pepper, chopped
1 tablespoon cilantro, chopped
2 tablespoons balsamic vinegar
1-ounce feta cheese, crumbled

Directions:

Put the fish in a roasting pan, brush it with 2 tablespoons oil, sprinkle salt and pepper all over and broil under medium-high heat for 15 minutes. Meanwhile, heat up a pan with the rest of the oil over medium heat, add the mushrooms, stir and sauté for 5 minutes.

Add the rest of the ingredients, toss, cook for 5 minutes more and divide between plates.

Top with the fish and serve right away.

Nutrition: calories 57

fat 23

fiber 12

carbs 23

protein 25

68) Sesame Shrimp Mix

Preparation time: 10 minutes

Cooking time: 0 minutes

Servings: 4

Ingredients:

2 tablespoon lime juice
3 tablespoons teriyaki sauce
2 tablespoons olive oil
8 cups baby spinach

14 ounces shrimp, cooked, peeled and deveined

1 cup cucumber, sliced

1 cup radish, sliced

¼ cup cilantro, chopped

2 teaspoons sesame seeds, toasted

Directions:

In a bowl, mix the shrimp with the lime juice, spinach and the rest of the ingredients, toss and serve cold.

Nutrition: calories 177

fat 23 fiber 12 carbs 23 protein 25

69) Creamy Curry Salmon

Preparation time: 10 minutes

Cooking time: 20 minutes

Servings: 2

Ingredients:

2 salmon fillets, boneless and cubed

1 tablespoon olive oil

1 tablespoon basil, chopped

Sea salt and black pepper to the taste

1 cup Greek yogurt

2 teaspoons curry powder

1 garlic clove, minced

½ teaspoon mint, chopped

Directions:

Heat up a pan with the oil over medium-high heat, add the salmon and cook for 3 minutes.

Add the rest of the ingredients, toss, cook for 15 minutes more, divide between plates and serve.

Nutrition: calories 402

fat 23

fiber 12

carbs 23

protein 25

70) Mahi Mahi and Pomegranate Sauce

Preparation time: 10 minutes

Cooking time: 10 minutes

Servings: 4

Ingredients:

1 and ½ cups chicken stock

1 tablespoon olive oil

4 mahi mahi fillets, boneless

4 tablespoons tahini paste

Juice of 1 lime

Seeds from 1 pomegranate

1 tablespoon parsley, chopped

Directions:

Heat up a pan with the oil over medium-high heat, add the fish and cook for 3 minutes on each side.

Add the rest of the ingredients, flip the fish again, cook for 4 minutes more, divide everything between plates and serve.

Nutrition: calories 402

fat 23

fiber 12

carbs 23

protein 25

71) Smoked Salmon and Veggies Mix

Preparation time: 10 minutes

Cooking time: 20 minutes

Servings: 4

Ingredients: 3 red onions, cut into wedges - ¾ cup green olives, pitted and halved

3 red bell peppers, roughly chopped

½ teaspoon smoked paprika

Salt and black pepper to the taste

3 tablespoons olive oil

4 salmon fillets, skinless and boneless

2 tablespoons chives, chopped

Directions: In a roasting pan, combine the salmon with the onions and the rest of the ingredients, introduce in the oven and bake at 390 degrees F for 20 minutes. Divide the mix between plates and serve.

Nutrition: calories 301 fat 23

fiber 12 carbs 23 protein 25

Vegetable

72) Vegetable Stew

Preparation Time: 10 minutes

Cooking Time: 25 minutes

Servings: 6

Ingredients

3 potatoes, peeled and diced

2 tomatoes, diced

2 carrots, chopped

2 small onions, finely chopped

1 zucchini, peeled and chopped

1 eggplant, chopped

1 celery rib, chopped

½ cup green peas, frozen

½ green beans, frozen

½ cup sunflower oil

1 bunch of parsley

1 tsp black pepper

1 tsp salt

Directions

In a deep saucepan, sauté the finely chopped onions, carrots and celery in a little oil.

Add in the green peas, green beans, black pepper and stir to combine. Pour over 1 cup of water, cover and let simmer.

After 15 minutes add the diced potatoes, the zucchini, the eggplant and the tomato pieces.

Transfer everything into an ovenproof casserole, sprinkle with parsley and bake for about 30 minutes at 350 F.

Nutrition: calories 343 fat 31 fiber 15 carbs 21 protein 23

73) Parmesan Broccoli

Preparation Time: 10 minutes

Cooking Time: 25 minutes

Servings: 4

Ingredients

2 Teaspoons Garlic, Minced

2 Tablespoons Olive Oil + More for Greasing the Baking Sheet

2 Heads Broccoli, Cut into Florets

1 Lemon, Zested & Juiced

½ Cup Parmesan Cheese, Grated

Sea Salt to Taste

Directions

Start by heating your oven to 400, and then get out a baking sheet. Grease with olive oil before setting it to the side.

Get a large bowl out and toss your broccoli with garlic, lemon zest, lemon juice, olive oil and sea salt.

Spread this mixture on the baking sheet. Make sure it's on a single layer, and then sprinkle with Parmesan cheese.

Bake for ten minutes. Your broccoli should be tender, and then serve warm.

Nutrition: calories 343

fat 31

fiber 15

carbs 21

protein 23

74) Roasted Vegetable Salad

Preparation Time: 10 minutes

Cooking Time: 25 minutes

Servings: 5

Ingredients

2 tablespoon olive oil

1 zucchini, cut into quarters

1 medium onion, cut into quarters

2 medium tomatoes, halve

2 red peppers, striped

1 medium eggplant, quartered

1 teaspoon garlic powder

2 mushrooms, cut into halves

Dressing:

1 teaspoon sumac

1 tablespoon apple cider vinegar

1 tablespoon lemon juice

2 tablespoons olive oil

4 tablespoons crushed walnuts

Directions

Preheat the oven to 490°F. Put sumac, lemon juice, vinegar and olive oil in a bowl and whisk.

Line a baking sheet with aluminum foil.

Put tomatoes, peppers, mushrooms, zucchini, onion and eggplant on the baking sheet.

Sprinkle with sumac mixture and roast for 25 minutes.

Serve and top with walnuts and add the dressing.

Nutrition: calories 344

fat 31

fiber 15

carbs 21

protein 23

75) Fried Green Tomatoes

Preparation Time: 10 minutes

Cooking Time: 8 minutes

Servings: 4

Ingredients

1 tablespoon Vegetable Oil

½ teaspoon Black Pepper

½ teaspoon Salt

½ cup Breadcrumbs

½ cup Cornmeal

1 cup All-purpose Flour

½ cup Milk

2 Eggs

4 Green Tomatoes

Directions

Pour the vegetable oil into a large pan and begin to heat it up into a medium heat.

While the oil heats, you will want to prepare your tomatoes by slicing them into half inch-thick pieces.

Be sure to throw the ends out as you will have no need for them. In a bowl, mix together the milk and the eggs.

Place your flour onto a plate and line up with the bowl that is holding the milk and eggs.

On a third plate, mix together your breadcrumbs, cornmeal, pepper, and salt.

Now that these are prepared, dip your tomato pieces in the liquid mixture, the flour, and then the breadcrumb mixture. Be sure to coat the tomatoes before tossing them into the vegetable oil.

Fry the tomatoes for five minutes on either side or until golden brown. Portion them out and enjoy as a side dish or a nice, healthy snack!

Nutrition: calories 322

fat 31

fiber 15

carbs 21

protein 23

76) One-of-a-Kind Veggie Slaw

Preparation Time: 10 minutes

Cooking Time: 20 minutes

Serves: 5

Ingredients:

2 tsp salt

2 tbsp Bavarian seasoning

½ cup lightly packed fresh mint leaves

½ cup fresh lemon juice

½ cup roasted and shelled pistachios, roughly chopped

6 oz dried cranberries

4 bacon strips, cooked to a crisp (keep rendered fat) and chopped to bits

1/3 cup extra virgin olive oil (use rendered fat from bacon to reach ½ cup)

2 lbs. Brussels sprouts, cleaned and trimmed of large stem pieces

Directions:

Shred Brussels sprouts in a food processor. Transfer into a large salad bowl.

In a small bowl mix salt, Bavarian seasoning, mint and lemon juice.

Then slowly add oil while whisking continuously and vigorously. Add more seasoning to taste if needed.

Pour half of dressing into the salad bowl, toss to mix and add more if needed.

Top salad with bacon pieces, dried cranberries and pistachios before serving.

Nutrition: calories 343

fat 31

fiber 15

carbs 21

protein 23

77) Ratatouille Grilled Style

Preparation Time: 10 minutes

Cooking Time: 20 minutes

Serves: 4

Ingredients:

2 tbsp walnuts, toasted and chopped

2 tbsp apple cider

2 tbsp extra virgin olive oil

2 medium yellow squash, cut into ¼" rounds

1 large zucchini, cut into ¼" rounds

1 large zucchini, cut into ¼" rounds

1 large Portobello mushroom cap, cut into ¼" slices

1 medium eggplant, cut into ¼" rounds

1 red bell pepper, quartered, stems and seeds removed

1 large red onion, cut into ¼" slices

Directions:

Preheat grill to medium high and lightly grease grill pan with cooking spray.

Place all sliced veggies in grill pan and drizzle with olive oil. Toss well to coat.

Place in grill and grill for ten minutes. Toss vegetables to ensure even heating and continue grilling for another 10 minutes.

Toss vegetables and check if lightly charred and cooked through. If needed, grill some more to desired doneness.

Transfer grilled veggies into salad bowl, add walnuts and zero belly dressing. T

Toss to combine well, serve and enjoy.

Nutrition: calories 343

fat 31

fiber 15

carbs 21

protein 23

78) Roasted Root Veggie

Preparation Time: 30 minutes

Cooking Time: 60 minutes

Serves: 6

Ingredients: 2 tbsp olive oil

1 head garlic, cloves separated and peeled

1 large turnip, peeled and cut into ½-inch pieces

1 medium sized red onion, cut into ½-inch pieces

1 ½ lbs. beets, trimmed but not peeled, scrubbed and cut into ½-inch pieces 1 ½ lbs.

Yukon gold potatoes, unpeeled, cut into ½-inch pieces

2 ½ lbs. butternut squash, peeled, seeded, cut into ½-inch pieces

Directions: Grease 2 rimmed and large baking sheets. Preheat oven to 425oF.

In a large bowl, mix all ingredients thoroughly.

Into the two baking sheets, evenly divide the root vegetables, spread in one layer. Season generously with pepper and salt.

Pop into the oven and roast for 1 hour and 15 minute or until golden brown and tender. Remove from oven and let it cool for at least 15 minutes before serving.

Nutrition: calories 298 fat 31 fiber 15 carbs 21 protein 23

79) Stuffed Sweet Potato

Preparation time: 10 minutes

Cooking time: 60 minutes

Serves: 4

Ingredients:

4 small sweet potatoes

15-ounce cooked black beans

1 cup corn

3 green onions thinly sliced

1/2 cup cilantro chopped

For the Vinaigrette:

2 limes juiced and zested

1/2 teaspoon salt

1/2 teaspoon ground black pepper

2 teaspoons honey

2 teaspoons adobo sauce

1 tablespoon olive oil

Directions:

Set oven to 350 degrees F and let preheat.

In the meantime, whisk together all the Ingredients: for vinaigrette until well combined.

Place sweet potato on a baking sheet and bake for 45 to 60 minutes or until fork tender.

Meanwhile stir together beans corn onion and cilantro in a bowl until mixed.

Pour in prepared vinaigrette and toss until combined set aside until required.

When sweet potatoes are roasted cut in half lengthwise and let cool for 15 minutes.

Push down in center of potato to create a divot by using back of a spoon and stuffed with prepared corn mixture. Serve straightaway.

Nutrition: calories 343

fat 31

fiber 15

carbs 21

protein 23

Meat

80) Mediterranean Grilled Pork Chops

Preparation time: 1 day

Cooking time: 20 minutes

Servings: 6

Ingredients:

2 pork chops

¼ cup olive oil

2 yellow onions, sliced

2 garlic cloves, minced

2 teaspoons mustard

1 teaspoon sweet paprika

Salt and black pepper to taste

½ teaspoon oregano, dried

½ teaspoon thyme, dried

A pinch of cayenne pepper

Directions:

In a small bowl, mix oil with garlic, mustard, paprika, black pepper, oregano, thyme and cayenne and whisk well.

In a bowl, combine onions with meat and mustard mix, toss to coat, cover and keep in the fridge for 1 day. Place meat on preheated grill pan over medium high heat, season with salt and cook for 10 minutes on each side.

Meanwhile, heat a pan over medium heat, add marinated onions, stir and sauté for 4 minutes.

Divide pork chops on plates, add sautéed onions on top and serve.

Nutrition: calories 234 fat 3 fiber 15 carbs 21 protein 23

81) Simple Pork Stir Fry

Preparation time: 10 minutes

Cooking time: 15 minutes

Servings: 4

Ingredients:

4 ounces bacon, chopped

4 ounces snow peas

2 tablespoons butter

1-pound pork loin, cut into thin strips

2 cups mushrooms, sliced

¾ cup white wine

½ cup yellow onion, chopped

3 tablespoons sour cream

Salt and white pepper to taste

Directions:

Put snow peas in a saucepan, add water to cover, add a pinch of salt, bring to a boil over medium heat, cook until they are soft, drain and leave aside.

Heat a pan over medium high heat, add bacon, cook for a few minutes, drain grease, transfer to a bowl and leave aside.

Heat a pan with 1 tablespoon butter over medium heat, add pork strips, salt and pepper to taste, brown for a few minutes and transfer to a plate as well.

Return pan to medium heat, add remaining butter and melt it. Add onions and mushrooms, stir and cook for 4 minutes.

Add wine, and simmer until it's reduced. Add cream, peas, pork, salt and pepper to taste, stir, heat up, divide between plates, top with bacon and serve.

Nutrition: calories 343

fat 31

fiber 15

carbs 21

protein 23

82) Pork and Lentil Soup

Preparation time: 10 minutes

Cooking time: 1 hour

Servings: 6

Ingredients:

1 small yellow onion, chopped

1 tablespoon olive oil

1 and ½ teaspoons basil, chopped

1 and ½ teaspoons ginger, grated

3 garlic cloves, chopped

Salt and black pepper to taste

½ teaspoon cumin, ground

1 carrot, chopped

1-pound pork chops, bone-in 3 ounces brown lentils, rinsed

3 cups chicken stock

2 tablespoons tomato paste

2 tablespoons lime juice

1 teaspoon red chili flakes, crushed

Directions:

Heat a saucepan with the oil over medium heat, add garlic, onion, basil, ginger, salt, pepper and cumin, stir well and cook for 6 minutes.

Add carrots, stir and cook 5 more minutes. Add pork and brown for a few minutes.

Add lentils, tomato paste and stock, stir, bring to a boil, cover pan and simmer for 50 minutes.

Transfer pork to a plate, discard bones, shred it and return to pan.

Add chili flakes and lime juice, stir, ladle into bowls and serve.

Nutrition: calories 343

fat 31

fiber 15

carbs 21

protein 23

83) Simple Braised Pork

Preparation time: 40 minutes

Cooking time: 1 hour

Servings: 4

Ingredients:

2 pounds pork loin roast, boneless and cubed

5 tablespoons butter

Salt and black pepper to taste

2 cups chicken stock

½ cup dry white wine

2 garlic cloves, minced

1 teaspoon thyme, chopped

1 thyme spring

1 bay leaf

½ yellow onion, chopped

2 tablespoons white flour

¾ pound pearl onions

½ pound red grapes

Directions:

Heat a pan with 2 tablespoons butter over high heat, add pork loin, some salt and pepper, stir, brown for 10 minutes and transfer to a plate.

Add wine to the pan, bring to a boil over high heat and cook for 3 minutes.

Add stock, garlic, thyme spring, bay leaf, yellow onion and return meat to the pan, bring to a boil, cover, reduce heat to low, cook for 1 hour, strain liquid into another saucepan and transfer pork to a plate.

Put pearl onions in a small saucepan, add water to cover, bring to a boil over medium high heat, boil them for 5 minutes, drain, peel them and leave aside for now.

In a bowl, mix 2 tablespoons butter with flour and stir well. Add ½ cup of strained cooking liquid and whisk well.

Pour this into cooking liquid, bring to a simmer over medium heat and cook for 5 minutes.

Add salt and pepper, chopped thyme, pork and pearl onions, cover and simmer for a few minutes.

Meanwhile, heat a pan with 1 tablespoon butter, add grapes, stir and cook them for 1-2 minutes.

Divide pork meat on plates, drizzle the sauce all over and serve with onions and grapes on the side.

Nutrition: calories 320

fat 31

fiber 15

carbs 21

protein 23

84) Pork and Chickpea Stew

Preparation time: 20 minutes

Cooking time: 8 hours

Servings: 4

Ingredients:

2 tablespoons white flour

½ cup chicken stock

1 tablespoon ginger, grated

1 teaspoon coriander, ground

2 teaspoons cumin, ground

Salt and black pepper to taste

2 and ½ pounds pork butt, cubed

28 ounces canned tomatoes, drained and chopped

4 ounces carrots, chopped

1 red onion cut in wedges

4 garlic cloves, minced

½ cup apricots, cut in quarters

1 cup couscous, cooked

15 ounces canned chickpeas, drained

Cilantro, chopped for serving

Directions:

Put stock in your slow cooker. Add flour, cumin, ginger, coriander, salt and pepper and stir.

Add tomatoes, pork, carrots, garlic, onion and apricots, cover cooker and cook on Low for 7 hours and 50 minutes.

Add chickpeas and couscous, cover and cook for 10 more minutes. Divide on plates, sprinkle cilantro and serve right away.

Nutrition: calories 216

fat 31

fiber 15

carbs 21

protein 23

85) Pork and Greens Salad

Preparation time:

10 minutes

Cooking time: 15 minutes

Servings: 4

Ingredients:

1-pound pork chops, boneless and cut into strips

8 ounces white mushrooms, sliced

½ cup Italian dressing

6 cups mixed salad greens

6 ounces jarred artichoke hearts, drained

Salt and black pepper to the taste

½ cup basil, chopped

1 tablespoon olive oil

Directions:

Heat a pan with the oil over medium-high heat, add the pork and brown for 5 minutes.

Add the mushrooms, stir and sauté for 5 minutes more.

Add the dressing, artichokes, salad greens, salt, pepper and the basil, cook for 4-5 minutes, divide everything into bowls and serve.

Nutrition: calories 320

fat 31

fiber 15

carbs 21

protein 23

86) Pork Strips and Rice

Preparation time: 10 minutes

Cooking time: 25 minutes

Servings: 4

Ingredients:

½ pound pork loin, cut into strips

Salt and black pepper to taste

2 tablespoons olive oil

2 carrots, chopped

1 red bell pepper, chopped

3 garlic cloves, minced

2 cups veggie stock

1 cup basmati rice

½ cup garbanzo beans

10 black olives, pitted and sliced

1 tablespoon parsley, chopped

Directions:

Heat a pan with the oil over medium high heat.

Add the pork fillets, stir, cook for 5 minutes and transfer them to a plate.

Add the carrots, bell pepper and the garlic, stir and cook for 5 more minutes.

Add the rice, the stock, beans and the olives, stir, cook for 14 minutes, divide between plates, sprinkle the parsley on top and serve.

Nutrition: calories 220

fat 31

fiber 15

carbs 21

protein 23

87) Slow Cooked Mediterranean Pork

Preparation time: 20 hours and 10 minutes

Cooking time: 8 hours

Servings: 6

Ingredients:

3 pounds pork shoulder - boneless

¼ cup olive oil

2 teaspoons oregano, dried

¼ cup lemon juice

2 teaspoons mustard

2 teaspoons mint, chopped

3 garlic cloves, minced

2 teaspoons pesto sauce

Salt and black pepper to taste

Directions:

In a bowl, mix olive oil with lemon juice, oregano, mint, mustard, garlic, pesto, salt and pepper then whisk well.

Rub pork with marinade, cover and keep in a cold place for 10 hours.

Flip pork shoulder and leave aside for 10 more hours.

Transfer to your slow cooker along with the marinade juices, cover and cook on low for 8 hours.

Uncover, slice, divide between plates and serve.

Nutrition: calories 320

fat 31

fiber 15

carbs 21

protein 23

88) Pork and Bean Stew

Preparation time: 20 minutes

Cooking time: 4 hours

Servings: 4

Ingredients:

2 pounds pork neck

1 tablespoon white flour

1 and ½ tablespoons olive oil

2 eggplants, chopped

1 brown onion, chopped

1 red bell pepper, chopped

3 garlic cloves, minced

1 tablespoon thyme, dried

2 teaspoons sage, dried

4 ounces canned white beans, drained

1 cup chicken stock

12 ounces zucchinis, chopped

Salt and pepper to taste

2 tablespoons tomato paste

Directions:

In a bowl, mix flour with salt, pepper, pork neck and toss.

Heat a pan with 2 teaspoons oil over medium high heat, add pork and cook for 3 minutes on each side.

Transfer pork to a slow cooker and leave aside. Heat the remaining oil in the same pan over medium heat, add eggplant, onion, bell pepper, thyme, sage and garlic, stir and cook for 5 minutes.

Add reserved flour, stir and cook for 1 more minute. Add to pork, then add beans, stock, tomato paste and zucchinis.

Cover and cook on High for 4 hours. Uncover, transfer to plates and serve.

Nutrition: calories 310

fat 31

fiber 15

carbs 21

protein 23

89) Pork with Couscous

Preparation time: 10 minutes

Cooking time: 7 hours

Servings: 6

Ingredients:

2 and ½ pounds pork loin boneless and trimmed

¾ cup chicken stock

2 tablespoons olive oil

½ tablespoon sweet paprika

2 and ¼ teaspoon sage, dried

½ tablespoon garlic powder

¼ teaspoon rosemary, dried

¼ teaspoon marjoram, dried

1 teaspoon basil, dried

1 teaspoon oregano, dried

Salt and black pepper to taste

2 cups couscous, cooked

Directions:

In a bowl, mix oil with stock, paprika, garlic powder, sage, rosemary, thyme, marjoram, oregano, salt and pepper to taste and whisk well. Put pork loin in your crock pot.

Add stock and spice mix, stir, cover and cook on Low for 7 hours. Slice pork return to pot and toss with cooking juices.

Divide between plates and serve with couscous on the side.

Nutrition: calories 320

fat 31

fiber 15

carbs 21

protein 23

90) Easy Roasted Pork Shoulder

Preparation time: 30 minutes

Cooking time: 4 hours

Servings: 6

Ingredients:

3 tablespoons garlic, minced

3 tablespoons olive oil

4 pounds pork shoulder

Salt and black pepper to taste

Directions:

In a bowl, mix olive oil with salt, pepper and oil and whisk well.

Brush pork shoulder with this mix, arrange in a baking dish and place in the oven at 425 degrees for 20 minutes.

Reduce heat to 325 degrees F and bake for 4 hours.

Take pork shoulder out of the oven, slice and arrange on a platter. Serve with your favorite Mediterranean side salad.

Nutrition: calories 224

fat 31

fiber 15

carbs 21

protein 23

91) Herb Roasted Pork

Preparation time: 20 minutes

Cooking time: 2 hours

Servings: 10

Ingredients:

5 and ½ pounds pork loin roast, trimmed, chine bone removed

Salt and black pepper to taste

3 garlic cloves, minced

2 tablespoons rosemary, chopped

1 teaspoon fennel, ground

1 tablespoon fennel seeds

2 teaspoons red pepper, crushed

¼ cup olive oil

Directions:

In a food processor mix garlic with fennel seeds, fennel, rosemary, red pepper, some black pepper and the olive oil and blend until you obtain a paste.

Place pork roast in a roasting pan, spread 2 tablespoons garlic paste all over and rub well.

Season with salt and pepper, place in the oven at 400 degrees F and bake for 1 hour.

Reduce heat to 325 degrees F and bake for another 35 minutes. Carve roast into chops, divide between plates and serve right away.

Nutrition: calories 320

fat 31

fiber 15

carbs 21

protein 23

92) Slow Cooked Beef Brisket

Preparation time: 10 minutes

Cooking time: 9 hours

Servings: 8

Ingredients:

6 pounds beef brisket

2 tablespoons cumin, ground

3 tablespoons rosemary, chopped

2 tablespoons coriander, dried

1 tablespoon oregano, dried

2 teaspoons cinnamon powder

1 cup beef stock

A pinch of salt and black pepper

Directions:

In a slow cooker, combine the beef with the cumin, rosemary, coriander, oregano, cinnamon, salt, pepper and stock. Cover and cook on low for 9 hours. Slice and serve.

Nutrition: calories 400 fat 31 fiber 15 carbs 21 protein 23

93) Mediterranean Beef Dish

Preparation time: 10 minutes

Cooking time: 15 minutes

Servings: 6

Ingredients:

1-pound beef, ground

2 cups zucchinis, chopped

½ cup yellow onion, chopped

Salt and black pepper to taste

15 ounces canned roasted tomatoes and garlic

1 cup water

¾ cup cheddar cheese, shredded

1 and ½ cups white rice

Directions:

Heat a pan over medium high heat, add beef, onion, salt, pepper and zucchini, stir and cook for 7 minutes.

Add water, tomatoes and garlic, stir and bring to a boil. Add rice, more salt and pepper, stir, cover, take off heat and leave aside for 7 minutes.

Divide between plates and serve with cheddar cheese on top.

Nutrition: calories 320

fat 31

fiber 15

carbs 21

protein 23

94) Beef Tartar

Preparation time: 10 minutes

Servings: 1

Ingredients:

1 shallot, chopped

4 ounces beef fillet, minced

5 small cucumbers, chopped

1 egg yolk

A pinch of salt and black pepper

2 teaspoons mustard

1 tablespoon parsley, chopped

1 parsley spring, roughly chopped for serving

Directions:

In a bowl, mix meat with shallot, egg yolk, salt, pepper, mustard, cucumbers and parsley.

Stir well and arrange on a platter.

Garnish with the chopped parsley spring and serve.

Nutrition: calories 244

fat 31

fiber 15

carbs 21

protein 23

95) Meatballs and Sauce

Preparation time: 5 minutes

Cooking time: 8 minutes

Servings: 4

Ingredients:

1 egg, whisked

1 teaspoon cumin, ground

1 teaspoon allspice, ground

¼ cup cilantro, chopped

A pinch of salt and black pepper

2 pounds beef, ground

1/3 cup breadcrumbs

Vegetable oil for frying

For the sauce:

1 cucumber, chopped

1 cup Greek yogurt

2 tablespoons lemon juice

1 tablespoon dill, chopped

Directions:

In a bowl, mix the beef with the breadcrumbs, egg, cumin, allspice, cilantro, salt and pepper.

Stir well and shape into medium sized meatballs. Heat a pan with oil over medium heat.

Add the meatballs and cook for 4 minutes each side. In a bowl, mix the yogurt with the cucumber, lemon juice and dill - whisk well. Serve the meatballs with the yogurt sauce.

Nutrition: calories 263

fat 31

fiber 15

carbs 21

protein 23

Dessert

96) Cold Lemon Squares

Preparation time: 30 minutes

Cooking time: 0 minutes

Servings: 4

Ingredients:

1 cup avocado oil+ a drizzle

2 bananas, peeled and chopped

1 tablespoon honey

¼ cup lemon juice

A pinch of lemon zest, grated

Directions:

In your food processor, mix the bananas with the rest of the ingredients, pulse well and spread on the bottom of a pan greased with a drizzle of oil.

Introduce in the fridge for 30 minutes, slice into squares and serve.

Nutrition: calories 136

fat 11.2

fiber 0.2

carbs 7

protein 1.1

97) Blackberry and Apples Cobbler

Preparation time: 10 minutes

Cooking time: 30 minutes

Servings: 6

Ingredients:

¾ cup stevia

6 cups blackberries

¼ cup apples, cored and cubed

¼ teaspoon baking powder

1 tablespoon lime juice

½ cup almond flour

½ cup water

3 and ½ tablespoon avocado oil

Cooking spray

Directions:

In a bowl, mix the berries with half of the stevia and lemon juice, sprinkle some flour all over, whisk and pour into a baking dish greased with cooking spray.

In another bowl, mix flour with the rest of the sugar, baking powder, the water and the oil, and stir the whole thing with your hands.

Spread over the berries, introduce in the oven at 375 degrees F and bake for 30 minutes.

Serve warm.

Nutrition: calories 221 fat 11.2 fiber 0.2 carbs 7 protein 1.1

98) Black Tea Cake

Preparation time: 10 minutes

Cooking time: 35 minutes

Servings: 8

Ingredients:

6 tablespoons black tea powder

2 cups almond milk, warmed up

1 cup avocado oil

2 cups stevia

4 eggs

2 teaspoons vanilla extract

3 and ½ cups almond flour

1 teaspoon baking soda

3 teaspoons baking powder

Directions:

In a bowl, combine the almond milk with the oil, stevia and the rest of the ingredients and whisk well.

Pour this into a cake pan lined with parchment paper, introduce in the oven at 350 degrees F and bake for 35 minutes.

Leave the cake to cool down, slice and serve.

Nutrition: calories 243

fat 11.2

fiber 0.2

carbs 7

protein 1.1

99) Green Tea and Vanilla Cream

Preparation time: 2 hours

Cooking time: 0 minutes

Servings: 4

Ingredients:

14 ounces almond milk, hot

2 tablespoons green tea powder

14 ounces heavy cream

3 tablespoons stevia

1 teaspoon vanilla extract

1 teaspoon gelatin powder

Directions:

In a bowl, combine the almond milk with the green tea powder and the rest of the ingredients, whisk well, cool down, divide into cups and keep in the fridge for 2 hours before serving.

Nutrition: calories 120

fat 11.2

fiber 0.2

carbs 7

protein 1.1

100) Blueberry Frozen Yogurt

Preparation Time: 15 minutes

Cooking Time: 30 minutes

Servings: 4

Ingredients:

1-pint blueberries, fresh

2/3 cup honey

1 small lemon, juiced and zested

2 cups yogurt, chilled

Directions:

In a saucepan, combine the blueberries, honey, lemon juice, and zest.

Heat over medium heat and allow to simmer for 15 minutes while stirring constantly.

Once the liquid has reduced, transfer the fruits in a bowl and allow to cool in the fridge for another 15 minutes.

Once chilled, mix together with the chilled yogurt.

Nutrition:

Calories per serving: 233

Carbs: 52.2 g

Protein: 3.5 g

Fat: 2.9g

101) Delectable Strawberry Popsicle

Preparation Time: 10 minutes

Cooking Time: 10 minutes

Servings: 5

Ingredients:

2 ½ cups fresh strawberry

½ cup almond milk

Directions:

Blend all ingredients until smooth.

Pour into the popsicle molds with sticks and freeze for at least 4 hours.

Serve chilled.

Nutrition:

Calories per serving: 35

Carbs: 7.7g

Protein: 0.6g

Fat: 0.5 g

102) Deliciously Cold Lychee Sorbet

Preparation Time: 10 minutes

Cooking Time: 5 minutes

Servings: 4

Ingredients:

2 cups fresh lychees, pitted and sliced

2 tablespoons honey

Mint leaves for garnish

Directions:

Place the lychee slices and honey in a food processor.

Pulse until smooth.

Pour in a container and place inside the fridge for at least two hours.

Scoop the sorbet and serve with mint leaves.

Nutrition:

Calories per serving: 151

Carbs: 38.9g Protein: 0.7g

Fat: 0.4

103) Easy Fruit Compote

Preparation Time: 10 minutes

Cooking Time: 15 minutes

Servings: 4

Ingredients:

1-pound fresh fruits of your choice

2 tablespoons maple syrup

A dash of salt

Directions:

Slice the fruits thinly and place them in a saucepan.

Add the honey and salt.

Heat the saucepan over medium low heat and allow the fruits to simmer for 15 minutes or until the liquid has reduced.

Make sure that you stir constantly to prevent the fruits from sticking at the bottom of your pan and eventually burning.

Transfer in a lidded jar.

Allow to cool.

Serve with slices of whole wheat bread or vegan ice cream.

Nutrition:

Calories per serving: 218

Carbs: 56.8g

Protein: 0.9g

Fat: 0.2g

104) Five Berry Mint Orange Infusion

Preparation Time: 15 minutes

Cooking Time: 10 minutes

Servings: 12

Ingredients:

½ cup water

3 orange pekoe tea bags

3 sprigs of mint

1 cup fresh strawberries

1 cup fresh golden raspberries

1 cup fresh raspberries

1 cup blackberries

1 cup fresh blueberries

1 cup pitted fresh cherries

1 bottle Sauvignon Blanc

½ cup pomegranate juice, natural

1 teaspoon vanilla

Directions:

In a saucepan, bring water to a boil over medium heat. Add the tea bags, mint and stir. Let it stand for 10 minutes.

In a large bowl, combine the rest of the ingredients.

Put in the fridge to chill for at least 3 hours.

Nutrition:

Calories per serving: 140

Carbs: 32.1g

Protein: 1.2g

Fat: 1.5g

105) Greek Yogurt Muesli Parfaits

Preparation Time: 10 minutes

Cooking Time: 10 minutes

Servings: 4

Ingredients:

4 cups Greek yogurt

1 cup whole wheat muesli

2 cups fresh berries of your choice

Directions:

Layer the four glasses with Greek yogurt at the bottom, muesli on top, and berries.

Repeat the layers until the glass is full.

Place in the fridge for at least 2 hours to chill.

Nutrition:

Calories per serving: 280

Carbs: 36g

Protein: 23 g

Fat: 4g

106) Mediterranean Baked Apples

Preparation Time: 15 minutes

Cooking Time: 25 minutes

Servings: 4

Ingredients:

1.5 pounds apples, peeled and sliced

Juice from ½ lemon

A dash of cinnamon

Directions:

Preheat the oven to 250°F.

Line a baking sheet with parchment paper then set aside.

In a medium bowl, apples with lemon juice and cinnamon.

Place the apples on the parchment paper-lined baking sheet.

Bake for 25 minutes until crisp.

Nutrition:

Calories per serving: 90

Carbs: 23.9g Protein: 0.5g

Fat: 0.3g

107) Spiced Pear with Applesauce

Preparation Time: 5 minutes

Cooking Time: 15 minutes

Servings: 4

Ingredients:

¼ Teaspoon Nutmeg, Ground

½ Teaspoon Cinnamon, Ground

2 Tablespoons Honey, Raw

¼ Cup Water

2 Tart Apples, Peeled, Cored & Chopped

1/8 Teaspoon Cloves, Ground

4 Pears, Peeled, Cored & Chopped

¼ Cup Water

Directions:

Place a saucepan over medium heat, adding in your ingredients. Cover the pan and bring it to a boil. Reduce the heat to low, cooking for twenty minutes. The fruit should soften. Remove it from the pot, and then mash until mostly smooth.

Chill before serving.

Nutrition:

Calories: 202

Protein: 1 Gram

Fat: 1 Gram

Carbs: 53 Grams

108) Cherry Clafoutis

Preparation Time: 15 minutes

Cooking Time: 30 minutes

Servings: 4

Ingredients:

2 Tablespoons Butter, Room Temperature

½ Cup Almonds, Unsalted & Ground

1 ¼ Cups Milk

2 Eggs

½ Cup Sugar, Divided

½ Cup All Purpose Flour

1 Tablespoon Vanilla Extract, Pure

3 Cups cherries, Pitted

1/8 Teaspoon Sea Salt, Fine

Directions:

Start by heating your oven to 350, and then get out a nine-inch pie pan. Brush it down with butter, sprinkling your ground almonds on the bottom.

Mix your milk, eggs, vanilla, ¼ cup of sugar, flour, and salt in a blender, pureeing until smooth.

Pour this batter into your pie plate and arrange your cherries over the batter. Sprinkle your remaining sugar on top and bake for thirty-five to forty-five minutes. It should be golden brown.

Allow it to cool for at least ten minutes before serving.

Nutrition: Calories: 407

Protein: 10 Grams Fat: 16 Grams

Carbs: 57 Grams

109) Stuffed Figs

Preparation Time: 10 minutes

Cooking Time: 10 minutes

Servings: 6

Ingredients:

20 Almonds, Chopped

2 Tablespoons Honey, Raw

4 Ounces Goat Cheese, Divided

10 Fresh Figs, Halved

Directions:

Start by preheating your oven's broiler to high.

Get out a baking sheet and place your figs with the cut side up. Sprinkle each with ½ teaspoon of goat cheese and a teaspoon of almond. Broil for two to three minutes, and then allow them to cool for five minutes before drizzling with honey to serve.

Nutrition: Calories: 209

Protein: 8 Grams Fat: 9 Grams

Carbs: 27 Grams

Health Benefits of the Mediterranean Diet

The Mediterranean diet is not about following a specific set of restrictions and rules in order to achieve your desired results. This alone makes it easier to follow than many diet plans because it is not really a diet plan at all but more of a way of life. The main idea behind the Mediterranean diet is to eat real food in reasonable quantities. And because it emphasizes the consumption of foods that are good for you, then it is reasonable that the Mediterranean diet has many health benefits to offer.

Following the Mediterranean diet might lower your risk of developing heart disease. Right now, heart disease is responsible for killing one out of every four Americans every year. You are more likely to die from some form of heart disease than you are to die from any other illness or accident. Some forms of heart disease are unavoidable, like congenital diseases that people are born with. But most forms of heart diseases are directly caused by or made worse by a sedentary lifestyle and poor dietary habits.

Many heart-related illnesses are caused by high blood pressure. Your blood pressure consists of two numbers: the systolic number and the diastolic number; the systolic number is the one on top. The diastolic number shows how much pressure your blood is putting on the walls of the arteries in your body when your heart is at rest in between its beats. The systolic number measures the amount of pressure the blood is putting on the walls of the arteries when your heart is beating. Once your systolic number is over one hundred thirty and your diastolic number is over eighty, you are considered to have problems in your blood pressure.

There are several factors that might cause your heart to pump harder to move blood throughout your body. One of these causes is obesity. Your body will create more miles of arteries to supply blood flow to the areas of your body that are larger than they are supposed to be. Then your heart will need to pump harder and more often to get the blood circulating through these arteries.

Another factor in high blood pressure is the buildup of plaque in the arteries. Plaque is made from calcium, cholesterol, and fat that is found floating in blood. These molecules will break off and float randomly through the bloodstream. They will likely become stuck on the part of the artery wall that has been damaged from thinning and thickening as blood was pumped through. Then the one molecule will catch other molecules as they float by, and soon, a plaque buildup will happen. When it does, the artery will become narrower, and the blood will need to be more forcibly pumped through in order to get past the blockage. The fat and cholesterol are byproducts of obesity.

When the flow of blood to and from your heart is blocked, for whatever reason, then you can suffer from a heart attack. A heart attack will happen when there is a blockage in one of the coronary arteries that brings the blood back to your heart when it is full of oxygen. If the blockage can continue for very long, then the muscles of the heart will begin to die. A stroke is much the same thing as a heart attack, except that it happens in the arteries that lead to the brain. Like the muscles of the heart, the muscles of the brain can quickly die if they are deprived of oxygen for too long. And just like a heart attack, the likelihood of suffering a stroke is increased with obesity.

Cholesterol is a compound that naturally occurs in the body. Your body uses it to make certain hormones, make cell tissues, and protect your nerves. Generally, your liver will make all the cholesterol that your body will need, but you will also get some cholesterol from your diet. Your overall cholesterol level is made of two numbers: your high-density lipoprotein (HDL) and lower-density lipoprotein (LDL). The LDL takes the cholesterol to various parts of the body, and the HDL removes unnecessary cholesterol from the body. Triglycerides are just a fancy name for the excess fat that your body stores for later use. Any calories that are not needed by the body when they are taken in are stored as fat for the body to burn for energy in between meals. When there is too much stored fat, the level of triglycerides in your body will be too high.

Diabetes can occur congenitally, such as Type One Diabetes, or it can be a product of poor lifestyle and obesity, such as Type Two Diabetes. The second form of diabetes, which is often referred to as sugar diabetes, relates more to how your body handles sugar and not how much sugar you eat. When you eat or drink, you are consuming sugar in some form and level. Some foods naturally contain more sugar than other foods. Fruit contains fructose, which is a natural sugar but still a type of sugar. When you consume something, your brain sends a message to your pancreas to create the hormone insulin to help break down the molecules from the food and help your body use them as energy. When your body has broken down the food, it has converted them to small molecules. Then the insulin will travel through the body with the food to help it get into the cells where it is needed.

When you continuously overeat or eat a large amount of processed and refined foods, the body will make more insulin to help the foods get into the cells for use as energy. The problem comes when this becomes a repeated cycle, where the pancreas needs to keep making more and more of the insulin. Also, over time, the cells in your body will become resistant to insulin when they are full and have no room for more molecules of energy. When that happens, the molecules will be stored as fat in various places in the body.

The risk of developing certain cancers, like pancreatic, kidney, esophageal, uterine, breast, and colorectal increases with obesity. This is believed to be the work of visceral fat surrounding the major organs of the body and affect certain necessary processes in the body. The cells of visceral fat are quite large, and there are many of them in the body of an obese person. One thing that visceral fat does is prevent oxygen-rich blood from getting to the organs in the amounts needed to sustain life. This environment that is low in oxygen causes a rise in inflammation. Some inflammation is good for the body. If you have a small scrape or a cut, then the body will send white blood cells to the area to kill any bacteria in the wound. This rush of white blood cells will cause inflammation to the area, a small swelling that will go away when the risk of infection is gone, and the white blood cells are no longer needed.

When your organs are surrounded by visceral fat, that area of the body increases in size. The body perceives this to be an inflammation caused by a foreign intruder, and it will send out its white blood cells to attack the intruder. This, in turn, will cause more inflammation. So, while the fat cells continue to divide and multiply, the white blood cells are trying to eliminate them. The cell division increases the chances that a tumor will eventually form.

Of all the forms of arthritis that people might suffer from, osteoarthritis is the most common. It is also known as the wear and tear form of arthritis since it often happens in joints that are used excessively, such as the hands and the spine, and in the knees and the hips—the weight-bearing joints. Osteoarthritis will often develop because of a genetic predisposition to developing arthritis or as the result of an injury to a joint. It is aggravated by obesity. In fact, being obese can increase the risk of developing arthritis. Just one pound of excess weight will put four pounds of extra pressure on weight-bearing joints.

And what do all these conditions have in common? That's right—obesity. Obesity develops when you have more weight on your body than you need. It is measured not just by your overall weight but also the ratio of your weight to your height, a number that is referred to as your BMI—body mass index. Your BMI is calculated this way:

BMI = height in inches divided by weight in pounds

So, if you weigh two hundred pounds, and you are six feet tall, then your equation would look like this:

72 / 200 = .36 or a BMI of thirty six percent

Anything over thirty percent is considered obese.

There is only one proven way to get rid of obesity, and that is to lose weight. This is where you will see the benefits of the Mediterranean diet. Because it is based heavily on plant nutrition, it is difficult to gain weight while on this diet. But, of course, it is possible. You might put too much olive oil on your food, for one, or you might still consume processed or refined foods. But if you follow the diet correctly, then you do not really have to worry about counting calories because most of the foods are naturally low in calories.

Look at it this way. One medium-sized carrot is about six inches long and no wider than one inch, and it has about twenty-five calories. There are roughly three thousand five hundred calories in one pound of body weight. So, this means that you would need to eat about one hundred forty carrots to gain one pound of body weight.

So, the bottom line is that the Mediterranean diet will help you to avoid or eliminate potentially fatal health problems simply by reducing your overall weight. It is not even all that difficult to do. These simple steps will make the Mediterranean diet successful for you:

Follow the recommended portion sizes.

Avoid refined sugar and flour.

Avoid processed foods.

Never skip breakfast.

Have vegetables and fruit in every meal.

Stay well-hydrated.

Eat whole grains.

Stay active.

By adhering to these steps, you will be successful at the Mediterranean diet. And do not worry about being bored. There are so many options and recipes to try that it may take a lifetime to try them all. And what a healthy life it will be.

Insider Secrets to Reaching Diet Success

How to Stay Hydrated

Once you've started and are fully immersed in the Mediterranean diet, you might notice that you've started to feel a little bit weak, and a little bit colder, than you're used to. The Mediterranean diet places an emphasis on trying to cut out as much sodium from your diet as possible, which is very healthy for some of us who already have high sodium levels. Sodium obviously is found in salt, and so we proceed to cut out salt – and then drink enough water to drain every drop of sodium from our bodies. When it comes to hydration, the biological mechanisms for keeping us saturated and quenched rely on an equal balance of sodium and potassium. Sodium can be found in your interstitial fluid, and potassium can be found inside our cytoplasm – two sides of one wall. When you drink tons of water, sweat a lot at the gym, or both, your sodium leaves your body in your urine and your sweat. Potassium, on the other hand, is only really lost through the urine – and even then, it's rare. This means that our bodies almost constantly need a refill on our sodium levels. But if you aren't eating any salt, or drinking any salt, then where are you supposed to get the salt that will help you stay hydrated? Plenty of individuals on the Mediterranean diet choose to manage their hydration through pills, instead of simply adding more salt back into their foods. This is a smart route, because sodium taken orally will make it to your blood stream faster. Now, if you're wondering exactly how much water you should be drinking, let's look at a sneaky little formula you can use to determine close to the proper amount of water you need. To start off, you're going to want to divide your weight in pounds by the number two point two. The equation should look something like this:

[Weight (lbs.)] / [2.2]

After that, you're going to want to multiply by the following dividends based upon your age group. If you're thirty or younger, multiply your number by 40. If you are between the ages of thirty and thirty-five, you should only multiply by thirty-five. Finally, if you're older than fifty-five, you should multiply your figure by thirty. Once you've worked your way through these steps, divide that sum by the number twenty-eight point three. The resulting number, likely in the thousands, is the number of ounces per day of water that you should drink for your age and weight. Ounces per day, unfortunately, is a bit of an unhelpful measurement – so you should divide that number by eight in order to determine the number of cups per day you need to drink.

Let's do an example. If you're thirty years old and weigh one hundred and thirty-five pounds, you will start by dividing one hundred and thirty-five by two point two. You get 40.61 After that, you will want to multiply that number by 40. Your number is now 2,454.54. This might seem astronomical, but remember, this measurement is in ounces. To get the number of cups per day, divided that number by thirty-eight, and you get 62.

If you're the type that like to keep up with a regular exercise schedule, you should try and drink an extra eight to twelve ounces of water daily, and at least two more glass than you would normally during a workout. The rule of thumb for strenuous activity is to drink an extra twelve ounces of water for every thirty minutes longer you're at the gym. While this is generally a great way to keep yourself hydrated, the best way by far is to listen to your body's signals.

Vitamins and Supplements

We touched a little bit earlier on how your body needs two crucial, wordy elements daily in your diet order to stay alive – crucial elements called "macronutrients" and "micronutrients". Macronutrients, which you know are your carbohydrates, fats, and proteins, supply your body with fuel to make energy, as well as help in our daily metabolic processes. In order to facilitate the best possible digestion and utilization of our macronutrients, you need your micronutrients – vitamins and minerals – to lend a helping hand. Vitamins and minerals can be found in plants and animals, yes, but often fruits and vegetables are much stronger sources. When consume another animal, we are consuming the sum of all the energy and nutrition that that animal has also consumed. This might sound like a sweet deal, but the pig you're eating used that energy in his own daily life, and therefore only has a tiny bit left to offer you. Plants, on the other hand, are first-hand sources of things like calcium, vitamin K, and vitamin C, which our bodies require daily doses of. You can choose to take a multivitamin to supply yourself with some of the basic vitamins and minerals that your body needs, but there are a few essential supplements that scientists know work well to augment a Mediterranean diet. Since you won't be eating that much red meat, (barely any if you have a lot of self-control), you should take an iron supplement with guidance from your doctor for a month or so before beginning the Mediterranean diet. Iron isn't something we need a constant supply of, but most regular adults are already deficient and could use a bit of help. Speaking of vitamins and minerals that we're already deficient in, vitamin D is essential for the strength of your bones as well as your absorption of calcium.

Meal Preparation and Portion Planning

If you haven't heard of the term "meal prep" before now, it's a beautiful day to learn something that will save you time, stress, and inches on your waistline. Meal prep, short for meal preparation, is a habit that was developed mostly by the body building community in order to accurately track your macronutrients. If you work a nine to five job like most of us, you know the struggle of feeding yourself a healthy dinner after work when you're tired, hungry, and just want to go home. When western society started getting more and more fast paced, we developed the fast food restaurant that could serve you from your car. While we all love to indulge in a little junk food now and then, fast food restaurants are marketed more towards routine family use than to a one-off indulgence. If you have kids, you're probably even more familiar with this struggle. Some of the members of the fitness community had finally had enough, and so they developed a way to cook healthy, homemade meals every single week without busting the bank, sacrificing time in the gym, or sacrificing time with your loved ones. The basic idea behind meal prep is that each weekend, you manage your free time around cooking and preparing all your meals for the upcoming week. While most meal preppers do their grocery shopping and cooking on Sundays, to keep their meals the freshest, you can choose to cook on a Saturday if that works better with your schedule. Meal prep each week uses one large grocery list of bulk ingredients to get all the supplies you need to make four dinners and four lunches of your choice. This means that you might have to a bit of mental math quadrupling the serving size, but all you must do is multiply each ingredient by four. Although you don't have to meal prep more than one meal with four portions each week, if you're already in the kitchen, you most likely have cooking time to work on something else. Many body builders even prep their breakfasts and on-the-go snacks during the weekend, to save time and make sure they know what they're eating. For the average person, meal prepping four dinners alone will already free up a ton of time during the week – for a gym session, perhaps, or more time relaxing with the family. When you cook for meal prep, you're going to be creating one meal in four portions – which can take up a lot of dishes. Investing in some good pots, pans, and skillets will help you work more efficiently in the kitchen, and matching Tupperware are something a good meal prepper can never resist. Once you've cooked your entire four-portion meal in one batch, you can separate out individual matching portions that you will eat throughout the week. Most cooked vegetables and meats can last for up to five days in the refrigerator, but you can feel free to freeze your entrees as well if you need the space. Vegetables that are uncooked normally have three to four days only, but that's why you're only reaching about four days in advance. If you want to keep your meals fresher for longer, you can always look for glass Tupperware with locking seals that can keep freshness in for longer. Each week, you can do repeat this process with new recipes and new ingredients. However, it's worth it to note that if you're someone who likes consistency, meal prepping might be a bit of an adjustment. Meal prep tends to make only one identical dinner meal and one identical lunch meal each week – which means that eaters who like to have a different dinner each night might have their work cut out for them. One of the easiest ways to combat this is by simply making a dinner and a lunch that can be interchanged whenever necessary to create variety. Once you've learned how to meal prep, you will save yourself enough time in the evenings relax, practice some self-care, and really extend your dinner hours to have fun conversation with friends and family. Now, meal preparation isn't just a cool technique to save you time and money – meal prep at its very core was designed to help you manage your weight loss in a convenient way, which is exactly what you need to succeed.

Tracking Your Macronutrients

Wouldn't it be nice if you could have a full nutritional label for each of your home-cooked meals, just to make sure that your numbers are adding up in favor of weight loss? Oddly enough, tracking your macronutrients in order to calculate the nutritional value of each of your meals and portions is as easy as stepping on the scale. Not the scale in your bathroom, however. A food scales! If you've never had a good relationship with your weight and numbers, you might suddenly find that they aren't too bad after all. Food scales are used to measure, well, your food, but there's a slick system of online calculators and fitness applications for your smart phone that can take this number and turn it into magic. When your meal preps each week, keep track of your recipes diligently. Remember how you multiplied each of the ingredients on the list by four to create four servings? You're going to want to remember how much of each vegetable, fruit, grain, nut, and fat you cooked with. While you wait for you meal to finish cooking, find a large enough plastic container to fit all your meal. Make sure it's clean and dry and use the empty container to zero out your scale. Once you've finished cooking your entire meal, transfer ALL FOUR PORTIONS into the clean plastic container and take not of the weight. When you use your online calculator or fitness app, you can enter the amount of each ingredient you used to cook the meal, and then the weight of the entire four portions. This will give you an estimate of how many carbohydrates, proteins, and fats are contained within each dish, and how many overall calories your meal comes out to be. Now, you're obviously not going to be consuming all of this at once, and so you will have to divide each number by four in order to get the proper readings. At the end of this process, you will have an almost entirely complete nutritional label for a meal that you made at home, from fresh and healthy ingredients that you know won't make you gain weight. It's one of the many ways that the Mediterranean diet turns something tedious like math and intimidating like scales into a delicious and nutritious way of living a healthier, and happier, life. Speaking of scales, let's talk a little bit about using the caloric estimates on your homemade meals to track your calories, and implicate a deficit, in order to lose more weight than you ever thought possible.

Counting Calories and Forming a Deficit

When it comes down to the technical science, there is one way and only one way to lose weight: by eating fewer calories in one day than your body requires to survive. Now, this doesn't mean that you can't lose weight for other reasons – be it water weight, as a result of stress, or simply working out harder. Although counting calories might not be the most fun way to lose weight, a calorie deficit is the only sure-fire way of guaranteeing that you reap all the weight loss benefits of the Mediterranean diet for your efforts. Scientifically, you already know that the healthy rate of weight loss for the average adult is between one and two pounds per week. Get ready for a little bit more math, but it's nothing you can't handle in the name of a smaller waistline. One pound of fat equals around thirty-five hundred calories, which means that your caloric deficit needs to account for that number, each week, without making too much a dent on your regular nutrition. For most of us, we're used to eating between fifteen hundred and two thousand calories per day, which gives you a blessedly simply five hundred calorie deficit per day in order to reach your healthy weight loss goals. If you cut out exactly five hundred calories each day, you should be able to lose one pound of fat by the end of seven days. Granted, this estimate does consider thirty minutes of daily exercise, but the results are still about the same when you rely on the scientific facts. If your age, height, weight, and sex predispose you to eat either calories per day, you might want to consult with your doctor about the healthiest way for you to integrate a caloric deficit into your Mediterranean diet. This is one of the handiest ways that weighing your meals on a food scale can help you lose weight. If you know the exact number of calories in each of your portions, you can be mathematically exact about your deficit – which is the only way to make it possible. The final most important benefit of counting your calories and weighing your food with a food scale is a psychological benefit, for you. When you take the time to weight out your meals and calculate your calories, it's highly likely that you will lose weight simply because of the math. This means that you don't have to weigh yourself every single morning just to track whether you're losing weight. If you know that the healthy level of weight loss for an adult individual is one to two pounds per week, you also know that it isn't necessary to obsess over the scale in the time periods that you're patiently waiting to drop pounds. Weight loss with a caloric deficit is guaranteed to happen – but you must be patient with real, healthy change. Weighing yourself once at the beginning of the week, in the morning on an empty stomach, and once at the end of the week, in the morning on an empty stomach, will give you a perfectly accurate snapshot of your weight loss (without the constant feeling that you aren't making progress). Counting calories doesn't have to be taboo, and it doesn't have to be anything other than science. Your weight loss should be yours, and you are entirely in control of your calorie count.

Frequently Asked Questions

Question: How effective is the Mediterranean diet for weight loss?

Answer: It's an effective diet for weight loss and maintenance, as part of a balanced way of eating and living. It's best to consider the benefits of the Mediterranean diet from a fuller, lifestyle-based approach, which includes exercise, relaxation, and meditation while enjoying balanced meals with whole foods. For rapid weight loss, adjusting to this diet works faster for some people, while others may take longer. Keeping active is an important aspect of this wat of eating and living, which should be incorporated at least three times a week for significant results.

Question: Is the low carb diet a compatible way of eating with the Mediterranean diet?

Answer: Some foods and nutrients are in common with both meal plans. Since the Mediterranean foods are generally rich in healthy fats and high in fiber, they can be easily incorporated into low carb eating habits. The food options for both diets are low in processed sugar, moderate in protein, and avoid process options. Unlike the Mediterranean diet, some versions of low carb include red meats and high levels of fat, while the Mediterranean is more moderate. While there are restrictions on the type and variety of fruits and vegetables to include in low carb diets, there are no limits to the Mediterranean meal plans.

Question: Are all fruits and vegetables suitable for a Mediterranean diet?

Answer: Yes, all fruits and vegetables are compatible with the Mediterranean way of eating. They are all nutritious, and while some varieties are more common in this diet because they are available in the Mediterranean, such as olives, greens, and certain fruits, any variety of plant-based food is welcome to include with ant variety of foods or recipe. This is an advantage because it is less restrictive while providing a healthy benefit to your health. The key is balance and eating reasonable portions with a variety of healthy foods.

Question: Is the Mediterranean diet generally approved by doctors and medical professionals?

Answer: Yes, and often the Mediterranean diet is preferred over other diets that are more restrictive towards limiting calories and/or carbohydrates. The Mediterranean way of eating has been around for many years with a lot of scientific research and studies to support its positive effect on health. Since all the nutrition requirements are included in this diet, there is no danger in deficiencies. There is a much better chance of avoiding deficiency of certain nutrients as a result of following this diet.

Question: Is red meat allowed as part of the Mediterranean diet?

Answer: In moderation, red meat is acceptable and included to some extent in some meals. This is because beef, pork, and other forms of red meat, when consumed too often and in large amounts, can contribute to heart disease and other medical conditions. In moderation and small amounts, lean cuts of red meat are excellent to enjoy with larger portions of vegetables and salads, as most Mediterranean meals focus on plant-based foods.

Question: Is it safe to modify the Mediterranean diet to a low-fat version?

Answer: It is possible, though it would not be recommended, as the facts contained in this diet are vital for good health and required to provide adequate nutrients. Not only will reducing fat decrease the nutrition of the diet, but it also will not guarantee a loss of weight and result in stronger hunger pains. For a diet to be sustainable and more than a short-term fix, it must provide all the required options. While many people look for quick diet options and results, any success they achieve will be undone once they revert to their old ways of eating.

Question: Is alcohol consumption allowed on the Mediterranean diet?

Answer: All foods and drinks are enjoyed in moderation, including alcoholic beverages. Dry red or white wine is recommended in small amounts, up to one glass per day, which can be beneficial to your health in moderation. Other alcoholic beverages, such as hard liquors, or mixed drinks high in sugar, should be avoided or enjoyed on occasion only.

Question: Is it easy to follow the Mediterranean diet while traveling?

Answer: When you consider the number of options available within the Mediterranean diet, there are plenty of options when traveling out of town, in a different country or region. Fortunately, there is no requirement for counting calories, or carbohydrates, which makes adapting to different types of cuisine easier to enjoy, without concerns about what to eat, if you keep in mind the following tips:

If you're visiting a coastal town, city, or resort by the ocean, you will have opportunities to enjoy fresh seafood and meals with fish as a feature in most cafes and restaurants. If dining out is expensive, consider local shops or street food vendors to taste test various treats and local foods.

Fresh fruit and vegetables are often available in local grocery shops or outdoor markets, especially if the weather is warm and you're traveling during the weekend. Enjoy local produce as much as possible, as they are more likely to be fresh and less contaminated. Become familiar with specialties of the region that provide healthy food options, to gain a better idea of what's available, and try different options.

Research online and contact different sources before you embark on your trip. Some destinations provide a surprising amount of variety in terms of cuisine and options for allergies, food sensitivities, and accommodations for various diets and needs. Many resorts and hotels are open to making special arrangements for guests who call or order ahead with their specific needs. If you want to ensure there are healthy foods available where you plan to stay on your vacation, making plans is the best option.

If you're going on a road trip, packing loads of snacks and healthy foods is a great idea for avoiding limited options in rural and remote areas and ensuring you have nutritious options for your vacation.

Question: Are there any types of foods that can be enjoyed as a deep-fried option?

Answer: Most foods can be prepared and enjoyed healthily, such as steamed, baked, lightly sautéed, or enjoyed raw. Deep frying, while it is a popular way to enjoy many foods from meat to seafood and vegetables, is the worst way to consume food, because of strips any nutritional value available, while adding dangerous carcinogens and trans fats that should be avoided to prevent many conditions and diseases that are harmful. Long term consumption of deep-fried foods can contribute to a higher risk of cancer, type 2 diabetes, and heart conditions. If you're currently eating deep-fried foods regularly, begin replacing them with healthier options, such as the following:

Replace French fries with mashed or baked potatoes

Choose a salad or soup instead of fried vegetables, fries or onion rings

Keep the consumption of hamburgers to a minimum and only prepare them with all-natural ingredients in your oven or stovetop.

Grilled vegetables or salads are a great way to enjoy a tasty fiber-filled side dish. They can be enjoyed with a baked salmon steak, pork chops, or roast chicken, instead of any deep-fried options.

Avoid pastries, donuts, and deep-fried desserts as much as possible, and instead, choose fresh fruits, homemade pudding, cookies, and cakes where you are aware of the ingredients.

Keep fresh fruits, nuts, and seeds on hand and on the go as snacks, to avoid the temptation of deep-fried and sugary snacks

Question: How much dairy is healthy on the Mediterranean diet or in general?

Answer: The quality of dairy products is just as important, if not more vital than the amount you consume. Yogurt is one of the most important options for dairy, and a popular choice for the Mediterranean diet. It's high in calcium, protein, and due to being fermented, yogurt contains a good source of probiotics, which is imported for balanced gut health. Choosing natural, unsweetened, and unflavored yogurt is the best option for good quality. This applies to other dairy products as well. Choosing cheese, milk, butter, and other dairy products from a local farmer or supplier is often the most likely way to have the best quality.

When it comes to quantity, dairy is often consumed in small to moderate amounts in the Mediterranean diet. It's important to choose from good sources while avoiding products with artificial ingredients or brands with negative publicity based on the quality of their goods and service provided. For example, factory farming results in mass production, which may be good for revenue, but takes away from the quality. Choosing dairy foods from a local farm with healthy practices, preferably where no preservatives are used, is ideal. This isn't always the easiest option, depending on where you live or shop. It's also important to avoid eating excessive dairy and to focus mainly on fresh vegetables and fruits. Dairy and meats should be a secondary option, and plant-based first, to create a healthy balance in your diet.

Question: How often is eating fish healthy?

Answer: Fish is the healthiest meat-based protein for your diet, and therefore it is an important part of the Mediterranean way of eating. It's a leaner source of protein than red meats and poultry, and it contains omega 3s and 6s, as well as calcium. If you have access to fresh, healthy sources of seafood, it's safe to enjoy daily, along with a good serving of plant-based foods. Olives, fruits (lemon or lime as a condiment), herbs, and seasoning are excellent options to enjoy with your serving of halibut, salmon, haddock or other type of fish.

Question: Are spices and seasoning options limited in the Mediterranean diet, or can they be applied often?

Answer: Spices and seasoning can be used liberally with any meal you choose, if you enjoy the flavor and have no allergies. Some people tend to limit the amount of salt, Sea salt is easier to absorb in the body than regular table salt, which makes it easier to tolerate. When people have high sodium levels, this is often due to processed foods, such as smoked meats, cheese, and other packaged foods that are full of preservatives. The regular, raw salt is good in moderation, or it can be omitted or reduced as required. Pink Himalayan salt is another great option to use for meals, and salt alternatives can be found in many natural food stores or markets where salt or sodium must be avoided entirely. By choosing natural foods without additives, this allows the option of adding or skipping the seasoning of any spice, including common options such as salt, pepper, and spices. In general, all spices and forms of seasoning are excellent for your health and add a great deal of taste to any dish.

Question: Which sweetener(s) are best to use for a healthy blood glucose level, and to avoid developing conditions such as type 2 diabetes or excessive weight gain?

Answer: Avoid refined sugars, sweeteners, and syrups, and instead, use natural forms of sugar, such as raw, coconut sugar, and maple syrup. Unless you follow a plant-based diet that prohibits all animal-based foods, honey can also be used as a natural sweetener. Even where natural options for sugar are used, it's best to use them sparingly, as they can spike blood glucose and change insulin levels. People following a low carb diet that avoids sugar altogether or as much as possible, swerve, monk fruit and other alternatives including erythritol are used. To accommodate these options for a variety of recipes, low carb sweeteners can be found in the form of icing sugar and syrups, for easier application.

Question: Is it safe to eat meat every day, including red meat and poultry? Are there benefits to limiting the amount of meat in the diet?

Answer: This is a personal choice for many people, to decide whether to follow a strict, plant-based diet, or to include all or some forms of meat or plant-based foods. There are many variations, all of which have advantages, whether it's adhering to a pescatarian diet (fish only, with no other added meats), a semi-vegetarian diet, where only poultry and/or seafood is included, but red meats are avoided, or a vegetarian diet where only dairy and/or eggs are included. There are many variations to these options based on personal motives and reasons. For all diets, it is important to limit the amount of red meat, because of the high fat and some of the effects pork and beef can have on increasing cholesterol, the risk of certain types of cancer, heart disease, and other conditions. When red meat is included in your diet, it is best to enjoy in a small or moderate portion, with the leanest cut available, and with a larger portion of fresh vegetables and/or fruits.

Question: Is olive oil best to consume raw instead of heated?

Answer: Olive oil, as with any natural oils, are an important, nutritional part of the Mediterranean diet. Enjoying them in their raw form is optimal for getting the most of their nutrients, though heating in a skillet or using for baking is acceptable in small amounts. Coconut oil and avocado oil are also healthy options to enjoy and can be used in place of olive oil. Heating oils at a very high temperature, such as deep-frying, and using oils with preservatives, can create toxins that can be dangerous. Minimizing the amount of heat change and choosing natural oils is key to balancing the benefits of oils in your diet and getting the most out of their value.

Question: Are dried fruits and vegetable or fruit chips healthy and acceptable for a Mediterranean diet?

Answer: Dried fruits and vegetables are good options, provided they are sun-dried instead of treated with chemicals. Vegetable and fruit chips are often available in grocery stores and convenience shops as an alternative to sodium-heavy potato chips and pretzels. While some may be well made and with minimal preservatives, it's important to avoid most brands as they can include high amounts of sodium and refined sugars. To ensure you're getting the most out of your diet, and the healthiest options, create your chips at home, using your oven or a dehydrator. Vegetable chips can take a few minutes or several hours, based on the sliced width and type of vegetable or fruit you are interested in creating into a chip. Kale chips, for example, are one of the easiest and quickest options to create, while zucchini or cucumber chips may take longer due to having a higher amount of moisture. If you plan on enjoying a wide range of both fruit and vegetable chips, it may be advantageous to invest in a dehydrator to create them.

Question: Is the Mediterranean diet one of the best ways to eat, or are there other, comparable diets that are similar?

Answer: In general, the Mediterranean diet is regarded as one of the most beneficial, as it focuses on nutrient balance and eating well, instead of counting calories and carbohydrates. For this reason, this way of eating can be considered more of a lifestyle than a diet, as it is not restrictive, and while there are foods to avoid and limit, there is no complete avoidance of any food types, as long as they are natural and without artificial ingredients and/or additives. Plant-based diets, low carb, and diet plans that focus on caloric restrictions may involve certain aspects of the Mediterranean diet, due to its many benefits, though there is no exact diet that can be considered better, only different, and more results-focused. For example, some people may follow a low carb diet to lose a significant amount of weight or reduce the symptoms of certain ailments or disease, while the Mediterranean diet focuses on good eating, healthy living and balance overall, with many of the same benefits shared with other diets and ways of eating.

Conclusion

The Mediterranean diet is a traditional diet that has roots that go back centuries. Indeed, the principles of this diet go back through time, well into the ancient past. People may have been eating this way from the very early days of agriculture thousands of years ago. Of course, they didn't have the insights that we do into the nature of human health. They didn't know about cholesterol, and many didn't live long enough to even develop heart disease, much less die from it. Simply getting enough food to eat was a challenge, and everyone was physically active because manual labor was necessary for survival. The diet developed as a result of the natural environment that existed around the Mediterranean region. The weather is perfect for growing olives and grapes, and the seas are rich in fatty fish. It was only natural that olive oil and red wine would become integral parts of the lifestyle of people and cultures living in this region.

Some also argue that the diet was consumed in the 1940s and 1950s simply as a result of the Second World War, which made processed food and meats harder to come by. There is some truth to this argument, but that is not a valid reason to avoid looking at the diet for its impact.

The reality is that the Mediterranean diet is timely; it is not out of date. At the present time, most people are suffering from health problems that are directly related to those that the Mediterranean diet solves. People are consuming large amounts of unhealthy, processed food. They often eat fast food that contains lots of sugars and corn syrup, along with unhealthy meat products. People are drinking sugary drinks and not getting the required amounts of fruits and vegetables. Many people never or rarely eat fatty fish.

Don't follow the old rule that you should only shop the perimeter of the grocery store. Today's supermarkets have Mediterranean Diet staples in every aisle—including the middle ones. While shopping, picture the Mediterranean Diet Pyramid inside your shopping cart: Half your cart should be fruits, vegetables, and plant-based foods, then fill up the rest with seafood, and so on.

Fresh produce section: What's in season? Seasonal fruits and vegetables are usually less expensive. Don't forget fresh herbs: Parsley, cilantro, basil, and mint can be budget-friendly ways to eat more always-in-season greens.

Fish counter: Ask questions. The fishmonger behind the counter is happy to steer you to inexpensive choices; he or she can also be a great source for recipes and cooking tips.

Canned fish aisle: There are lots of new additions here, including packets of tuna and salmon that are ready to eat with a fork. Most of the choices are simple and sustainable. Just pick your favorite or try something new, like sardines.

Frozen food aisle: The frozen food aisle is an ideal place to finish filling your cart with fruit and veggies. In general, frozen fruits and vegetables are just as nutritious as fresh, as they are frozen at the peak of freshness. Choose any vegetable without sauce. We buy frozen fruits to go into every breakfast, from cereal to yogurt. Frozen fish fillets are healthy, convenient choices, and because they're often frozen individually, you can cook just what you need.

Rice and grains aisle: In general, you'll find most whole grains here, in the natural food's aisle, or in the bulk food section. To make sure the grains are whole, search for these words on the Nutrition Facts label: oats, bulgur, wheat berries, rye berries, or whole [name of grain], such as whole wheat. Look for faro, bulgur, quinoa, sorghum, spelt, barley, brown rice (instant and regular), and wild rice without any added flavors or seasonings.

Bulk food section: This area, with foods in open bins, makes food shopping fun. Here's where you can buy small amounts of things to taste, without spending a lot on full packages of whole grains, beans, and dried fruits.

Dairy case: From low-fat to full fat, we promote eating the type of milk, cheese, or yogurt that you prefer. Products with more fat will have more calories, but we find that they are more filling and flavorful, and often you can use less in a recipe. When it comes to yogurt, we prefer plain, but if you are buying flavored yogurt, compare the amount of added sugar to other flavored yogurts and go with the lowest number. (The total sugar amount on the label also includes the lactose and fructose—those naturally occurring sugars found in dairy and fruit.) Or better yet, buy the plain and add your own fruit.

Made in the USA
Monee, IL
07 July 2020